dedication

To Sean, my Warrior Hero:

Thank you for loving me with courage,
Pursuing my heart with passion,
Challenging me to know God better,
And making life bigger than I ever dreamed.

I love you.

brio devotional series

by kathy wierenga buchanan

TYNDALE

Tyndale House Publishers, Inc.
Wheaton, Illinois

WANT MORE? LOVE

A Focus on the Family book
published by Tyndale House Publishers, Wheaton, Illinois 60189

Focus on the Family books are available at special quantity discounts when purchased in bulk by corporations, organizations, churches, or groups. For more information, contact: Focus on the Family, 8605 Explorer Drive, Colorado Springs, CO 80920; or phone (800) 932-9123.

Editor: Lissa Halls Johnson
Cover photography and design: Sally Leatherman
Interior design: Jeff Lane/LegacyRoad

Interior photography
Tiffany Derck: 5, 7, 8, 9, 18, 20, 23, 32, 33, 34, 35, 36, 39, 57, 61, 66, 70, 71, 72, 74, 77-80, 87, 93, 95, 99, 100, 107, 110-115, 117, 118 (top), 120, 121, 126-130, 137-146, 151
Jeff Lane: 16, 28, 30, 45, 47, 50, 59, 60, 109, 123, 125, 147, 149, 150
Laura Burt / Life Expressions: 152-155

Printed in Korea.
1 2 3 4 5 6 7 8 9 / 09 08 07 06 05 04

Contents

GOD'S POEM

Gabriel swallowed
his bite of
cheeseburger.

love

"So how's your day been, Gabriel?" asks Michael. The two sat across from each other at the Golden Gate Diner.

Gabriel swallowed his bite of cheeseburger. "Great. I watched God create a girl today. It was so exciting! She's so funny. And talented. She has this amazing compassion. She's going to reflect God's love for others. He really poured His heart into her."

"I love how His eyes light up when He finishes one of His creations."

Gabriel laughs. "know. I loved hearing Him talk about His 'Poem'—that's what He calls them."

Michael snatched one of Gabriel's fries. "But I don't get it. He knows they're going to disappoint Him. They always do."

The other angel nods, his eyes saddening. "He knows they're flawed. But He hopes that their failures will draw them to seek a relationship with Him. That's what He wants most of all. Can you imagine? God wants a relationship with this girl more than anything."

"I've known God for an eternity and I still can't grasp how much He loves His creations."

Gabriel took a sip of Dr Pepper. "I know. It's amazing. And the 'Created' don't get it either. They try so hard to do everything right, afraid that He'll turn His back on them for messing up. They don't get that they can't earn His love. He loves them simply because they're His. Because He created each one individually, He loves each one individually."

"Even when they hurt Him." Michael wipes away some ketchup that had smeared on his cheek. "He always forgives them. Her worth to the Almighty isn't based on how much she does right or wrong."

Gabriel nods. "But The Enemy sure knows how to convince them otherwise."

"It's too bad, "Michael says, musing. "Because God just wants them to come to Him, to know Him, and see the truth of how much He loves them."

love

It's not in your Bible quite like that. But it's there in a little different way. Read over the following verses and write out—in your own words—what God thinks about you. Don't skim over them quickly. Let them soak in. These are God's words written to you—His beloved.

Zephaniah 3:17

....
....
....

Psalm 139:13

....
....
....

Psalm 139:16b

....
....
....

Psalm 139:17-18a

....
....
....
....

Psalm 103:2-5

....
....
....
....
....
....

beloved

created

valuable

personal

dance

beloved

created

valuable

personal

dance

Now look at one more . . .

We are God's workmanship, created in Christ Jesus to do good works, which God prepared in advance for us to do. (Ephesians 2:10)

....

....

....

....

....

In the original Greek, the word *workmanship* is *poiema*, which is where our word *poem* comes from. Think about what it means to be a poem. You're not a piece of furniture on God's factory assembly line. You're a poem. When you think of a poem, what comes to mind? Write your thoughts here:

....

....

....

....

....

....

....

....

....

....

....

"Hey, Derek." I slid into the seat across from him. The normal bustle of the Student Union surrounded us. "Whatcha up to?"

Derek quickly covered his notebook with his arm. "Just writing a poem."

Derek had shared his poems with me before. His poems reflected personal aspects of his heart: his dreams, his desires, his ways of seeing the world. And because they were so personal, he didn't share them with just anyone.

"Can I see it?"

"It's not totally done yet, but I guess so."

He slid the notebook across the table, and I began to read. I loved his use of words and knew he had painstakingly chosen each one. His word pictures captivated me and there was a melodic quality to his phrasing. The poem gave me a new picture of the way Derek saw things and who he was as a guy.

Imagine God writing your life. It tells us in Psalms that each day was written before it came into being. God painstakingly chose the perfect combination of traits, talents, and desires to place in you. Creating your sense of humor, your way of seeing the world. Concentrating on your beauty. And, in all of it, placing in you a reflection of Him— unique just to you. No one reflects God's personality in the same way you do. You were designed as an outpouring of who God is. A unique, priceless, amazing combination of His character traits. A precious and delightful reflection of God's emotion.

Now look at the second part of Ephesians 2:10. He knew "in advance"—from the beginning of time—what your purpose would be. He's given you the unique gifts and personality that you need to accomplish His plans. He designed you specifically to be a reflection of Himself in every situation. Whether it's to counsel, mother, write, paint, dance, encourage, serve, speak, perform, or whatever, He made you with your purpose— His plan—in mind.

So how would Derek feel if I didn't appreciate his poem? He'd be disappointed and hurt, because it wouldn't be just the poem I'm degrading—I'd be demeaning him, too. Don't you think God must feel the same way when people don't see you as the precious girl He's made you to be? And how must God feel when the poem doesn't appreciate itself?

....

....

....

What do you, as a poem, think of how God "wrote" you?

....

....

....

....

....

....

....

a special prayer

Father, thank You for making me the way You have. Thank You for designing me specifically and uniquely to reflect You. Wow, God, how awesome it is to think that I represent the Creator and Ruler of the universe. Forgive me when I don't appreciate the way You "wrote" me. Lord, I offer You all my insecurities about the way I look or what I see as my lack of talent or significance. I give those to You, God, and ask that You fill me with Your vision for me. Help me to see myself the way You see me. Amen.

love

journal

DADDY TO THE RESCUE

love

Crisp orange, red, and yellow leaves canopied over the road and crunched under my tires, but I barely noticed. My thoughts replayed the worst moment of my life—a horrible, awful phone call that had taken place earlier that afternoon.

"I just wanted to let you know that unfortunately you were not chosen to receive the scholarship." The words had brought a knot to my throat. I'd counted on this scholarship. That's how I was going to afford college. How would I attend now? The conversation had been short. I "uh-huhed" through the rest of it, trying not to break out into tears over the phone. I didn't know what I was going to do for tuition money now.

And when I'd rather be curled up on my bed crying, I was on my way to baby-sit Carlie—the most hyperactive five-year-old you'd ever want to meet. I wasn't looking forward to it, but I'd promised her parents weeks ago that I'd watch her. As I pulled into her driveway, my somber moment was broken. Carlie sat perched on her front porch, waiting for me. She wore a purple sombrero, her dad's tie, and clown pants from an old Halloween costume. In one hand she held a bright yellow kite with a black smiley face design. I had to laugh.

"See my kite?"

"That's a great kite."

Her mom and dad bustled through the door for their afternoon out. "We'll be back in a couple hours, Princess." Her dad swung Carlie around and planted a kiss on her forehead. "Be good for Kathy."

We waved as they pulled out of the driveway. "I'm a princess," announced Carlie. "And I want to fly my kite."

The Saturday afternoon was perfect for kite-flying. Carlie laughed as the wind picked up the yellow toy and carried it through the blue autumn sky. She ran around trees and the house, trying to make it go higher and higher. It

...I'd rather be curled up on my bed crying.

worst

awful

knot

smiley

kiss

worst

awful

knot

smiley

kiss

didn't matter if the string was only 10 feet long; to her it was the highest-flying kite ever.

But as she stumbled backward over a rock, the string yanked from her hand. Mr. Smiley Face soared on his own up into the sky, looping circles as we tried in vain to capture him. Finally, the upper branches of an old oak tree caught hold of the string. We both stood at the bottom of the tree staring up into its branches. I knew one thing for sure: I wasn't about to climb up there and untangle it. That was way higher than I wanted to be.

I looked up at the kite, wondering what I would do to appease a disappointed little girl. I waited for her to break into tears. But she only sighed and said matter-of-factly, "Don't worry. My daddy will take care of it."

Look up Mark 14:36. What does Jesus call God in this passage?

....

This Aramaic word is literally translated as "daddy" or "papa."

And here's the cool part . . .

For you did not receive a spirit that makes you a slave again to fear, but you received the Spirit of sonship. And by him we cry, "Abba, Father." The Spirit himself testifies with our spirit that we are God's children. (Romans 8:15-16)

Can you believe it? God is *our* "Daddy."

Look up the following verses and note the results of being one of "God's kids":

Matthew 7:9-11:

....

....

Deuteronomy 8:5:

....

....

Romans 8:17:

....

....

love

questions:

I have a friend who prays to "Daddy." When I first heard it, I thought it seemed too informal. But the more I know of it, the more it seems appropriate. Even God-pleasing. *Daddy*.

Carlie's daddy rescued her kite within moments of returning home. And she was thrilled, but not at all surprised. She knew he would. She had every confidence that her daddy loved her enough to take care of her, and had the ability to do what was impossible for her.

I wish I had that confidence in my Abba. Human dads fail us. They sometimes don't love us as much as we need to be loved. They really can't do everything—even though we might think so when we're little. But my Daddy in heaven can. He really does know everything and He can do anything. When problems become too big, I don't need to know what to do. It's not my problem to fix. It's my Daddy's. And even with my college finances, He provided. Maybe next time I'm faced with a situation that looks impossible, my response will be like Carlie's: "Don't worry. My Daddy will take care of it."

What do you want to ask your Daddy to take care of right now?

....

....

....

....

....

....

....

....

....

....

....

....

a special prayer

Father, You are my Abba. My Daddy. I acknowledge that You love me, and that You desire the very best for me. Sometimes I forget that You're in control. Sometimes I don't trust how much You love me. Please forgive me for that. You know all my hurts, and You feel my sadness. Daddy, I don't know how and I don't know when, but I believe You'll help me through all my pain and confusion today. I release it to You. I know You'll take care of it. Thank You for loving me and making me Your daughter. I love You. Amen.

STUCK AT A SHEEP-CROSSING

They seemed to have no concept of danger.

Emerald-colored hills rolled past us as our tour bus traveled over a country road in Scotland bearing me and two friends on a journey to see one of Scotland's well-known castles.

Screech!

The bus halted.

"What is it?" I asked my friend Laura, who sat by a window.

Laura craned her neck out the open window to see around the front of the bus.

"Sheep," she said.

Sheep?

"They're crossing the road." Laura leaned farther out the window. "Sit tight. It looks like it's going to be a while."

That was the first of several "sheep" stops that day, and gradually, we got used to them. Swarms of woolly creatures filled the road, while a few shepherds attempted to prod them across. I learned sheep are not smart animals. They may be cute, warm, and fuzzy—but they are not bright.

The sheep wandered in circles until their shepherd set them straight. They seemed to have no concept of danger. Even after the shepherd prodded and poked them in the right direction, they'd only move a few steps before getting turned around and wandering the wrong way again. The shepherds had to prod the sheep with their staffs repeatedly. Imagine a hundred sheep with ADHD trying to cross a road and you can understand why it was such a long process. I had a new respect for the caretakers who tended them. *Can you imagine having that much patience?*

It's interesting that the Bible often uses sheep and shepherd imagery to illustrate our relationship with God. I hope the point is not that we're stupid, but that in the grand scheme of things we *are* pretty clueless. We need a Shepherd to watch over us and guide us along the way.

dig deeper

Today, let's take a look at some of these references to being the sheep of our heavenly Shepherd. Grab your Bible, and start by turning to John 10. Read verses 1-4.

What does this tell us about the Shepherd?

....
....
....
....

What does this tell us about the sheep?

....
....

How does this relate to our Christian walk?

....
....
....
....

Now read verses 14, 15 and 18 of the same chapter. What does this tell us about the Shepherd?

....
....
....
....

danger

wrong

prod

poke

patience

danger

wrong

prod

poke

patience

How is this like what Christ did for us?

....
....
....

I'm going to give you a couple more passages to think about. The first is in Psalm 23. You've probably heard these verses a number of times before, but they're worth looking at again.

The Lord is my shepherd, I shall not be in want. He makes me lie down in green pastures, he leads me beside quiet waters, he restores my soul. He guides me in paths of righteousness for his name's sake. Even though I walk through the valley of the shadow of death, I will fear no evil, for you are with me; your rod and your staff, they comfort me.

Isn't that comforting? If we follow our Shepherd, He leads us to places of rest and nourishment. We're not there all the time—sometimes we go through the dark valleys. But He will always lead us through them into better places. We can follow Him without fear. He is good. Take a look at the words *rod* and *staff*. Isn't it interesting that both are mentioned? A rod is a symbol of authority and was used to discipline the sheep. A staff, a pole with a crook at the end of it, was used to gently prod the sheep, and also to lift them out of crevices or other places they might be stuck. But it says in this passage that *both* the rod and staff are "comforting." One is to discipline and one is to rescue, but they both show the Shepherd's love.

Okay . . . last passage. Look up Matthew 18:12-14. What do these verses tell us about how much the Shepherd loves His sheep?

....

....

....

....

....

....

....

....

....

quiz time!

Are you ready to test your knowledge? Remember what you just learned about a shepherd and, using the words on the right, fill in the blanks in the sentences in the box below.

The shepherd _____ the sheep from wild animals.

The sheep know the shepherd's _____.

The shepherd knows the sheep by _____.

The shepherd _____ each sheep so much, he will go out hunting for a sheep that is lost.

The shepherd _____ the sheep in the direction they should go.

The shepherd leads the sheep to places of _____ and _____.

The shepherd's _____ is comforting, because he desires to protect his sheep.

The shepherd is willing to _____ his life to protect the sheep.

nourishment

name

sacrifice

guides

voice

rest

protects

discipline

loves

Now use the same words to fill in truths about you and your Shepherd.

God _____ my soul from things that would harm me for eternity.

I read God's Word so I can recognize God's _____.

God knows me by ____·_____ and everything about me.

God _____ me so much, He'll come after me if I wander away from Him.

God _____ me in the direction I should go and the choices I make.

If I follow God, He will lead me to places of spiritual _____ and _____.

God's _____ is comforting, because it shows His love.

Jesus was willing to _____ His life for me.

a special prayer

Father, thank You for being my Shepherd. I know sometimes I wander around in circles, but I know that You love me even then. Thank You for protecting me, guiding me, and giving Your life for me. Thank You for coming to find me when I get lost. Your love amazes me, God, and makes me want to love You even more. Teach me to recognize Your voice and follow You as closely as I can. Amen.

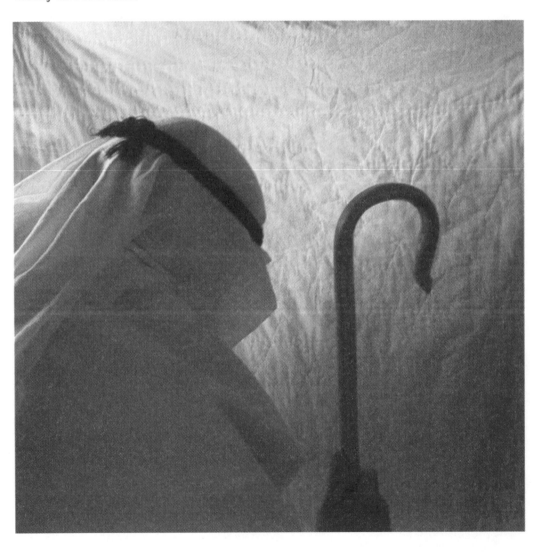

journal

PRINCESS ANNALEIGH AND THE NIDGITS

"You're stupid and ugly. You aren't worth much."

Once upon a time, in a beautiful kingdom, there lived a princess named Annaleigh. A great king ruled the kingdom. He resided in a palace in the center of the land, surrounded by many princes and princesses. All of his children were welcome to come see him at the palace anytime they wished.

The Princess Annaleigh went often to visit with the king. She'd sit on his lap while he told her stories. Sometimes they'd sing together.

When she wasn't in the palace, the princess loved to be outdoors. She'd splash in the stream running around the edge of the kingdom, climb the giant trees, and dance barefoot in the lush green meadows.

However, the Nidgits also lived in the kingdom. The Nidgits wanted to overthrow the Great King so they could rule the kingdom themselves. But they knew the Great King was too wise, too strong, and too powerful to be beaten. So they decided the best way to attack him was through his

children, and Princess Annaleigh became one of their targets.

The Nidgits knew that if the princess saw them, she'd pay no attention to them or what they said, so they decided to hide in the bushes while she waded in the river, climbed the trees, and danced in the meadow and tell her lies.

Beginning the following day, when Princess Annaleigh went out to play, she began to hear the whispered Lies. As she waded, she'd hear, "You're stupid and ugly. You aren't worth much." As she climbed, she'd hear, "The Great King doesn't really love you." As she danced, she'd hear, "The other princesses are prettier than you."

Sadly, Annaleigh began to believe the words. She felt worthless, unloved, and ugly. And she soon stopped wading, climbing, and dancing. But the words continued to ring in her head. She heard them over and over again. And they became more and more true to her. She also stopped visiting the Great King—*after all,* she thought,

love

why would he want to see stupid, ugly, worthless me?

One day, Princess Annaleigh heard a knock on the door. She'd hoped it wasn't one of the other princesses or princes asking her to play again. She was so tired of giving excuses. *Maybe I'll just ignore it,* she thought. But the knocking persisted, and she finally opened the door—just a crack. There, on her stoop, stood the Great King.

"Where have you been?" he asked, his voice soft and sad.

The Great King? Here to see me? But why?

She shrugged in response. She was ashamed to say that she wasn't worth it. That he had no reason to love her. That the other princesses were prettier than she.

But he seemed to know anyway. "My sweet Annaleigh, don't believe the Lies you hear whispered

sing

splash

dance

ashamed

sad

sing

splash

dance

ashamed

sad

by the Nidgits. They are not true. They only tell you those things to get you away from me."

The princess began to weep. And the Great King drew her into his magnificent arms and assured her of his love for her and her immense value to him.

The more she heard his voice, the more ridiculous the Lies seemed. Of course, they weren't true. She was precious. She was loved. She was beautiful.

The Great King looked solemn for a moment. "Annaleigh, the Lies will always be there. They will continue to be whispered around you. But you must come to me in order to know the truth."

The next day, Princess Annaleigh went to wade in the sparkling stream, climb the towering oak trees, and dance barefoot in the lush green meadows. The whispers still came. And the Lies seemed to make sense again. So she ran to the palace to see the Great King. And as he held her on his lap and stroked her hair, he spoke Truth to her until the Lies faded away, and once more she knew how much the King adored her.

love

questions:

Do you ever find yourself feeling like Princess Annaleigh when she heard the Lies?

....

What lies do you hear? Do you think you're too fat, too unattractive, too stupid to be loved? Write the lies below:

....

....

....

....

....

Where do the lies come from? Check all that apply.

_____ Magazines

_____ TV

_____ Other people

_____ Your own perception of yourself

_____ Movies

What else?

....

love

The Bible is the best place to find truth. According to Ephesians 6:17, it is the sword of the Spirit. Swords are used to defend oneself against attack. When the devil attacks us with lies, we can defend ourselves with the Word of God. Write out the following verses. Choose to memorize one this week, and fling the truth back at the devil when he throws lies in your direction.

Romans 8:38-39

....
....
....
....
....
....
....

John 16:33

....
....
....
....
....

Psalm 18:2-3

....
....
....
....
....
....
....
....

love

a special prayer

God, thank You for loving us so much that You gave us a Book of Truth to defend us. Please give me strength to fight against the lies of the Enemy. Your truth is all that is real. When I'm tempted to believe the lies, please help me be honest with You, so that You can share Your truths with me. Amen.

A MINOR ACCIDENT

I didn't just
do this.
I didn't just
do this.

It had been a good night at youth group, and I was feeling especially pleased since my parents had recently given me permission to drive myself there and back in Mom's brand-new Ford Taurus. All the way home, I reminded myself to use my turn signals, my mirrors—everything I'd been taught in Driver's Education a few months prior.

Upon arriving home, I carefully maneuvered the new car into the garage, imagining how pleased Mom would be when she saw my great parking job. I shifted into park and noticed if I inched the car forward a little further, I'd leave more room to walk behind the vehicle. I pressed my foot firmly on the brake as I shifted the Taurus into drive.

SHREEK!

CRASH!

Instead of moving forward a few inches, the car had lunged several feet, smashing through the back wall of the garage and into my sister's bedroom.

I didn't just do this. I didn't just do this.

I repeated the mantra in my head as I banged my forehead on the steering wheel. I took a deep breath, then looked up to see my sister's stuffed teddy bear eyeing me curiously from the bed.

I'd done it.

Why do they put the gas and brake so close to each other? They're so easy to confuse.

Maybe it's all a dream.

Maybe I'll wake up and discover this never happened.

Then my father's shocked voice assured me I was completely awake. "Kathy, what did you do?"

A bleak future flashed before my eyes.

I wouldn't be able to go to college next year because it would take all my savings to rebuild the house. I'd end up having to work at the local 7-11. I'd have to bike since I'd be grounded from borrowing the car until I became menopausal. Then one day while working, someone would come in to steal a Hershey bar and I'd get shot during the burglary. My life was essentially over.

love

questions:

Have you ever thought your life was "over"? When?

....

....

....

What happened in the end?

....

....

....

I wonder if Joseph in the Old Testament thought his life was over when his brothers sold him into slavery. We know the Israelites thought life was over when they saw the Red Sea in front of them and the charging Egyptians behind them. "Was it because there were no graves in Egypt that you brought us to the desert to die?" I'm sure they felt like I did—abandoned by God.

I don't know why bad things happen. A good friend dies, my boyfriend and I break up, I didn't get the scholarship I'd set my heart on. Each time, I cried feeling like life could never continue. But somehow it always did.

I spent several weeks my freshman year of college mourning the break-up of a longtime relationship. But as I look back on it now I think, *Praise God.* If we had stayed together, I wouldn't have grown and changed the way I have. I'd be living in a different part of the country in a different job and never know what I'd be missing. But God allowed the relationship to end because He had something (and someone) better for me. It's hard to see at the time. It's as if we can see one little piece of this big puzzle, and we have no idea what the picture is. But, gradually, over time, God shows us His plan. He reveals what He did in us and through us because of the unexpected, unplanned events.

What's a current disappointment in your life?

....

....

....

....

Look up the following verses and write what it tells us about keeping a God perspective.

Proverbs 3:5: ....

....

....

....

Psalm 41:5: ....

....

....

Job 37:5: ....

....

....

Psalm 27:13-14:...

....

....

....

What does it mean to keep a "God perspective" in your situation?

....

....

....

In the end, insurance covered all the damage to the house. My parents were pretty cool about letting me drive the car again. (Although my mom's hair turned gray shortly after.) My dad and I had a good time together repainting the new wall. And I never had to take a night job at the 7–11. Hmmm, I guess it wasn't such a tragedy after all. Funny how that works.

love

a special prayer

God, thank You for giving me hope. Thank You that my true hope is eternal life. That's better than anything I could have here—even if everything did go right. God, I pray that You will fill me with the hope that's in You. Protect me against getting discouraged and wanting to give up. I want to persevere for Your honor and glory. Amen.

love

journal

LEARNING TO LOVE, PART 1

She was making life miserable for me...

Lishayna would be a handful. I knew it within 10 minutes of meeting her.

The rest of the eight- and nine-year-old campers gathered around me that first day, eager to hear about what we'd do that week and nervous about being away from home. The camp where I worked ministered to children who lived below the poverty level. Funded by local churches, the camp allowed kids to come at practically no cost. Many of these girls had never been away from home for a week, but they were excited about the games, swimming, canoeing, and hiking that promised to fill the week ahead.

Well, except Lishayna. Although she was small for her age, she was the most intimidating nine-year-old I'd ever met. Her natty cornrows bristled as I explained the rules. She stared me down with squinted eyes and a permanent scowl across her face.

As we discussed the living arrangements in our cabin, I told the girls we'd settle disagreements, like who gets what bunk or who gets to be first in line, with the traditional game of Rock, Paper, Scissors. This seemed to work well with many of the campers as they chose beds. Until Lishayna's turn. She and Kiana faced each other, pounding their fists with "Rock" for the first three counts. On her fourth beat, Kiana hit her open palm with "Paper." On Lishayna's fourth beat, she hit Kiana in the face.

Needless to say, Kiana got the top bunk she wanted and Lishayna got a talking to. I explained to Lishayna that's not how we behave at camp. She lost her swim time that day as a consequence of her action, and I thought the two of us had an understanding.

I was wrong.

Over the next few days, Lishayna tried my patience in countless ways. She was caught stealing a hairbrush from another girl, using foul language, and kicking a staff member. She ran off on a regular basis, making me go on many Lishayna hunts. She threw sticks during Bible study, refused to clean up after dinner by dumping her plate on the floor, and complained endlessly about not being able to watch TV. The other counselors and I started referring to her as "The World's Smallest Monster."

What else could I do? After Lishayna had lost her swim time, evening snack, and canoeing time three days in a row, I didn't know what else to take away. And I was completely worn out.

God, how can I love this girl? I prayed one night. She was making life miserable for me and the other campers. *You have to help me with this. I can't do it on my own.*

eager

nervous

excited

behave

foul

eager

nervous

excited

behave

foul

Maybe it was in that moment when I felt completely emptied of everything good and strong inside me that God knew, "Now I can go to work." I woke up the next morning refreshed, and ready to take on The World's Smallest Monster. I felt renewed patience and a genuine compassion for Lishayna that had been lost under all the frustration and anger she caused me. But it wasn't from me—and I knew it. The love I felt was more than my human heart was capable of. *God was in me.*

love

Look up 2 Corinthians 4:6-9. Read it through twice, and then let's dig into it.

In verse 6, what is the light that God puts in our hearts? ....

....

That's kind of a long way of saying God's glory is in us. Think about that: The God who has infinite love and strength and wisdom dwells in us! He offers us His glory—the glory of His character and power. Only God had the love to care for an unlovable child like Lishayna, but He gave that to me!

According to verse 7, where do we keep God's glory (His treasure)? ....

....

....

....

Clay jars don't have a lot of outward value. They're easily breakable and aren't even very interesting to look at. That's kind of like me when I tried to care for Lishayna out of my own strength. I didn't have much to offer, but God fills the "jars of clay" with His treasure—and that's what gave me the strength to love beyond how I've ever loved before. Isn't that awesome? God put the best into what is most mundane. Once I humbled myself before Him—emptied out this clay jar, so to speak—He could fill me with Himself.

Why does God use "jars of clay"? Look at the last part of verse 7. ....

....

....

....

....

love

questions:

God deserves the praise for what He does! When I had nothing left to give, I relied on my heavenly Father's strength. And I knew that everything that came out of me from that point on was purely from Him. It wasn't me.

Can you think of people in your life whom God wants you to love, but you don't think you have it in you? Maybe your little sister is driving you crazy. Or maybe you're helping teach a Sunday school class and one of the little kids is really hard to love. Or your dad is having a hard time at work and you're getting the brunt of his frustration. Or maybe a friend is struggling with depression and you feel like running the other way. Ask God to reveal the situations where He wants to show His love through you. Write them below:

....

....

....

....

....

love

a special prayer

Father, thank You for filling me with Your love. Help me to pour that love and compassion onto those around me. Fill me with Your love, God, in each of the situations above. Help me to love each of those people with Your love. I admit that I can't do it without You. Thank You, God. Amen.

LEARNING TO LOVE, PART 2

My mom never wanted me. That's why she gave me away.

I don't know if Lishayna was tired on Thursday, but for once she seemed to listen to the campfire songs. She didn't participate, but she wasn't disruptive, either. By now I'd trained myself to keep one eye on her at all times, and I noticed her staring continuously at the orange flames. When the camp director rose to give the evening's talk, Lishayna became antsy. Looking around to see if anyone was watching, she ducked into the darkness of the trees. Exhausted, annoyed, and frustrated, I was on her tail.

About a hundred feet from the campfire circle, I caught up with her.

She turned. Arms folded. Scowl in place.

God, please help me.

"Lishayna, what do you want from me?"

A fire came into her eyes. "Stop pretending like you care so much!" She screamed so loud I wondered what the kids at campfire would think.

"I'm not pretending."

"Whatever."

I'm not sure where the idea came from. "Rock-paper-scissors you for it."

"What?" She looked as confused as I felt. But I maintained an expression that said it was perfectly normal to judge how much someone cared about you by playing rock, paper, scissors. "Oh, fine," she gave in.

I won 12 games in a row. I don't know how. No . . . I do.

"That doesn't prove anything. It's just a stupid game," she said.

But I knew I had her attention. "Well, then, you need to give me a reason for why I shouldn't care about you."

"I run away, I don't care about your stupid rules, I don't like you or the other girls—" She went on and on with the list. And all her reasons were

true.

"Do you know why I care about you, Lishayna?"

She shook her head.

"Because one day God looked down on this earth and said, 'I want a little girl named Lishayna. And I'm going to love her so much. No matter what she does I'm going to love her.' And He created you and brought you to camp this week. You're a gift from God. And I think that makes you worth caring about."

"That's a lie. No one planned me. My mom never wanted me. That's why she gave me away." She talked about being in a foster home, her third one that year. There were six other kids in the house. Her foster dad drank and yelled a lot.

I heard many stories that night—many of which broke my heart. She didn't seem like the world's smallest monster anymore. She was a little girl—a little girl who needed so much love. "God wants you," I told her. "And there's nothing you can do to make Him change His mind."

Things didn't change that night. But Lishayna went to sleep after complaining for only 15 minutes that night, instead of her usual 40. I went to sleep praying I could be God's vessel pouring His love into this little girl's life.

The rest of the week, I nurtured Lishayna. I told her Jesus' truths and I loved on her—hugging her, encouraging her, laughing with her. I knew the Enemy was still at work. But I knew my Father was bigger.

That Saturday I put her on the bus, promising I'd pray for her. Though I didn't keep in touch with Lishayna, I prayed for her throughout that year, pleading with God to protect her—to place her in a home where she would be loved and adored and treated like the precious little girl she was.

But was that enough?

trained

noticed

flames

love

sleep

trained

noticed

flames

love

sleep

questions:

Have you ever felt helpless in a situation? Like you couldn't do enough? Explain that situation: ....

....

....

....

How did you handle it? ....

....

....

dig deeper

One of my favorite passages is in Isaiah 61:1-3. Look it up. What are some of the things God calls us to do? ....

....

....

....

These are ways that you reflect God's love to others. Seems like a pretty big task, doesn't it? But before you give up, take a peek at 1 John 4:16. What does this tell us about love?

....

....

....

....

We are not the source of love. God is. And it is only when we are filled with His lavish love that we can pour it out on other people. What an honor!

I didn't know what to do for Lishayna. I hated that bad things were happening to her, and there was little I could do about it. As I look back, I believe I did what God called me to do in that time and place. I reported the abusive foster father, loved on Lishayna as I "bound up the brokenhearted"—but I didn't do it on my own. I brought her to my Father—the only One who could redeem her situation—and let Him give me the strength to love and care for Lishayna. He gave me the words to say. And He also gave me the assurance that even when I stepped out of the picture of Lishayna's life, He would continue to watch over her. I don't know where Lishayna is today, but I still believe that God is with her.

None of these things I did are possible without God. He doesn't intend for us to do them on our own. We first fill ourselves with Him so that we can offer comfort, love, and hope in a way that changes lives. God will bring people into your life who are hurting. Don't be afraid of that. Let His love flow through you. And when you've done what you can, remember God is still at work. And He can do anything.

Take a minute to think about friends who are hurting. Write their names below:

....

....

....

....

....

love

a special prayer

Father, thank You for giving me the love to love others with. Please show me the people in my life who I can love for You, and give me the strength and wisdom to do that well. God, right now I bring before You the people I know who are hurting. Lord, please heal their hearts. Show them Your love. Show them Your love through me. And thank You that even when I can't do anything else, You're still in control of their lives and love them even more than I do. In Your name, Amen.

love

journal

LEAPS IN LIFE

...to go through with it suddenly seemed far crazier than it did before...

Why in the world did I decide to do this?

It was a little late to ask the question. Already the single-prop plane was thousands of feet up in the air. And I was going to jump out of it. This was something I'd always talked about doing, but to go through with it suddenly seemed far crazier than it did before.

Drifting clouds simmered in the summer's heat. Tiny trees and homes peered up at me through the window of the noisy aircraft. Ribbons of high-ways made lines through the brown fields. And I was going to be floating down to them in a few minutes.

I shifted, feeling the weight of the attached pack. My tandem partner explained that he was hooking me in, adding words of assurance that each of these clips was strong enough to hold a Volkswagen. And I'm thinking, *How would they know? When was the last time a Volkswagen went skydiving?*

Then came the moment of truth. With the wind plastering my cheeks back and the huge Sangre de Cristo mountain range merely a blot beneath my feet, I stood on the tiny five-inch platform. The powerful rush of air tried to blow me back inside, while the plane engine drowned out any sound. Would I choose to jump or get back in the plane?

Before I tell you, grab your Bible and read Matthew 14:22-33.

love

I wonder if Peter felt the way I did as he stood on the side of the boat, with Jesus walking on the water toward him. The wind whipped the boat, drowning out the sounds of everyone around him. The disciples trembled, fearing that the figure moving toward them was a ghost.

And Jesus said, "Take courage, it is I. Do not be afraid."

Peter called out his recognition of Christ. And Jesus responded with one very significant word. "Come!"

The storm-tossed waves must have looked frightening. Yet Peter hopped out of the boat. What a crazy thing for him to do. Most likely, Peter didn't know how to swim. Truly, he took a leap of faith.

I took my leap too, right out of that plane into thin, cold air. My stomach lurched into my throat, and I plummeted downward at 90 miles per hour, until my chute opened (thankfully!) and I floated to the ground.

The parachute came to my rescue, and I had faith it would or I'd never have jumped in the first place. Peter had immense faith in Christ to want to do the terrifying impossible, trusting that his God-friend could rescue him.

God requires that same leap of faith from you. Maybe not out of a plane or a wave-flung boat, but He does ask you to do things that may seem risky or impossible.

Where does God want you to take a leap in your life and trust him? Does it mean changing friends? Changing habits? Asking for help? Risk looking stupid? Standing up for your beliefs? Going on a missions trip? Loving someone who's unlovable? Starting a Bible study at your school?

Remember, Jesus is saying the same thing to you that He did to Peter: "Take courage, it is I. Do not be afraid."

questions:

What leaps of faith is God calling you to make right now?

....

....

What fears are keeping you from making these leaps? ....

....

....

....

love

Look up Matthew 17:20, Matthew 19:26, and Philippians 4:13. What do these verses tell you about taking risks for God?

....

....

....

....

....

Is God big enough to rescue you when you take your leaps of faith? ....

....

....

love

a special prayer

God, You tell us that with You everything is possible. Forgive me for not having the faith to take the "leaps" You want me to take. God, I'll never know what You can do through me unless I give You the chance to show me. Help me serve You with courage. I want to see what You can do. In Jesus' name, Amen.

love

HEALING HIS DAUGHTER

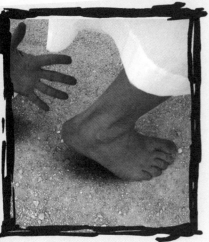

The woman bit her lip, her face flushing with heat. He knows.

Her chance had come—and it could be her last.

The woman had struggled with her illness for 12 years. She bled—every day—and it wouldn't stop. She'd traveled to many doctors hoping that *someone* might be able to help.

But no one could.

Then she heard about a teacher named Jesus. The town had been abuzz about this man who told stories and performed miraculous healings. Maybe, just maybe, *He* could heal her.

She hung on the edge of a jostling crowd waiting for Him to come. The crowd hummed with excitement. Voices called to one another as people relayed miracles they'd heard about or witnessed.

And then she saw Him. Her stomach jumped to her throat. The woman thought she'd burst with anticipation. But then, a ruler from the synagogue ran up to Jesus and flung himself onto the dirt in front of Him.

"Please, Jesus," the man, Jairus, cried. "My daughter is sick and on the verge of death. Please, please save her. Don't let her die."

Jesus lifted Jairus to his feet and said something to him, and the two started down the road.

The crowd pressed in to follow, eager to see the little girl be healed.

The woman's heart saddened, hope draining away. She wasn't the beloved daughter of a religious leader. And Jesus' time was too valuable to be wasted on the likes of her. Still, she let herself be caught up in the crowd.

Then the thought came to her. *He must have great power! Maybe . . . if I could just touch His cloak—* She weaved about the crowd's jagged edge then ducked into the thick of it to get closer to the Teacher. *This way I won't bother Him. He can go about His day doing important things for important people.*

She reached out. Closer . . . closer . . . then her hand skimmed across the hem of His cloak.

Jesus stopped. He turned. The woman froze.

"Who touched Me?" He asked.

The people must have thought the question ridiculous. Everyone had been close to Jesus. Lots of people had inadvertently touched him.

The woman's heart raced.

"Who touched Me?" Jesus asked again. "Someone touched Me; I know that power has gone out from Me."

The woman bit her lip, her face flushing with heat. *He knows.* She couldn't pretend it wasn't her and slink away. Trembling, she fell down before Him. "I'm sorry, Sir. I so desperately needed to be healed. Although I know I don't deserve it."

A lump in her throat kept more

bled

doctors

abuzz

sick

daughter

bled

doctors

abuzz

sick

daughter

words from coming. What would He do to her? One didn't go around touching respected Jewish rabbis—especially a bleeding woman. "I'm sorry," she choked.

And then she realized it. The bleeding had stopped. Stopped! She felt whole. Her body felt new. "I'm healed, Jesus," she whispered, looking up. "I'm healed!"

Jesus smiled. "Daughter, your faith has healed you. Go in peace."

Warmth and acceptance flooded through her. *Daughter. He called me "daughter."*

Daughter. **What a powerful word. Not "sinner" or "sneak" or "cowardly cloak-toucher."**

Do you see the picture? Jesus used the endearment of *daughter* to let the woman know how valuable she was to Him. He took the example of Jairus's deep love for his daughter . . . a father who cared little about his stature and respectability when it came to his daughter.

Jesus was saying to her, *I love you as this father loves his daughter. I sacrifice for you. I plead on your behalf. I do whatever it takes to protect and provide for you. I know what you need. And I will do everything in My power to make you whole.*

Think about your own dad. Circle some of the words that describe him:

Distant	Angry	Loving	Gentle	Passive
Uncaring	Good listener	Affectionate	Caring	Helpful
Protective	Hurtful	Encouraging	Godly	Fun
Wise	Unpredictable	Adventurous	Harsh	Busy

Other words? _____

Write the words from above that come to mind when you think about how God relates to you: ....
....
....
....

Do they overlap? ....
....
....
....

When we hear of God as "Father," we tend to think of our earthly fathers. Some of you may have fathers that are neglectful or seem disinterested, making you think of God as neglectful and disinterested. Others of you may have fathers who absolutely adore you and always look out for your best interest. If so, you probably have a pretty good perspective on God.

So, is Father God distant and busy, bothered by your problems? Or is He a Daddy who stands close to you—who longs to comfort you and hold you and watch over you?

God *adores* you. He can't get enough of you. He is always close to you—even when it doesn't feel that way. He is a Dad who delights in you. He wants to know about—and be *involved* in— every part of your life. He loves to hear your heart. He loves it when you laugh and enjoy life. He loves to spend time with you. He is a Dad who is concerned about the guys that you go out with, not because He's strict and possessive, but because He wants you to have the very best. He wants men to treat you right because He knows how much you deserve it.

Take a minute right now to pray that God would show you who He *really* is. Pray that He would remove any false beliefs about His character and replace them with truth.

dig deeper

Read Luke 8:40–48. What are some ways Jesus showed the woman in the story a father's love for a daughter? ....

....

....

....

Read Matthew 6:26 and 1 John 3:1. What do these verses tell us about our Father's love for His little girls? ....

....

....

....

....

a special prayer

Dear Father, I'm so thankful to be Your daughter. You're the Lord Almighty and You adopted me! I want to crawl up on Your lap and feel Your hugs. I want to walk with You hand in hand. I have the greatest title of all time as Your beloved princess. Thank You for blessing me with such an honor. Amen.

love

journal

love

IS GOD ANTI-MASCARA?

The concept of beauty is drilled into us from pigtail stage to denture days.

I stood in the bathroom, my face inches from the mirror. Propped up next to me on the counter was a magazine article titled "Shape Your Perfect Nose." I stuck my imperfect nose close to the article, studying the illustrated diagram. I *knew* that if I could just make my pudgy nose look smaller, I'd be a knockout. Surely, everyone who approached me was so stunned by its enormity, they could barely see the rest of me. And here the article was going to help me by giving me six simple steps to camouflage this huge flaw.

#1 Apply foundation to entire face. *Done.*

#2 Draw line with light highlighter from bridge of nose to tip. *Okay . . .*

#3 Shade both sides of nose with bronzer one shade darker than foundation. *Whoa . . .*

#4 Highlight divots above nostrils with light concealer. *Hmmm.*

#5 Darken the right side of right nostril and left side of left nostril. Highlight in between. *Is that right?*

#6 Draw attention away from nose by applying blush at 45-degree angle from apple of cheek to temples. *That can't be right.*

The whole point was to camouflage my nose. But trust me, if someone walked into the bathroom at that moment, all they would *see* was my nose—hideously striped in light and dark, with highlights and bronzer. *Oh, well . . .*

Why is how we look so

questions:

important? We want to have thin bodies with thick hair. Wide eyes with a narrow nose. A noticeable smile with not-so-noticeable skin flaws. The concept of beauty is drilled into us from pigtail stage to denture days. But how does a Christian woman deal with all that pressure? Let's go see what God has to say about it in 1 Peter 3:3: *Your beauty should not come from outward adornment, such as braided hair and the wearing of gold jewelry and fine clothes.*

So what's that mean? Is God saying we should try to be ugly? Was I supposed to stop wearing makeup? Never wash my hair? Trade in my cute sundresses for garbage bags with arm and leg holes cut out of them?

What do you think?..
....
....
....

Check out a few of these verses. Write out what you think God is saying about beauty.

Psalm 27:4 ....
....

Ecclesiastes 3:11 ....
....

Ezekiel 20:6 ....
....

God created beauty. He created sunsets and autumn leaves and a million different kinds of flowers. He formed mountains, designed sunsets, and invented tiger lilies. He decorated the dark sky with spectacular stars, embellished trees with colorful leaves, clothed lions in magnificent manes. He didn't have to do those things. What purpose do lilacs serve except to add beauty? Why don't leaves stay brown all year long? Because God, the Grand Artist, wanted to decorate the world for your enjoyment. God instructed that His temple be made and adorned using the finest linens, expensive woods, and elaborate gold overlayings—not just gray cinderblock. He wanted

His temple to be beautiful. And according to 1 Corinthians 6:19, *you are now His temple.*

And don't forget, God created *you* as beautiful, too! But don't think the beauty comes from the right lipstick or eyeliner, because it goes far deeper. A new haircut and outfit may accentuate your physical appearance, but they don't make you beautiful. That's what Paul is saying here: Don't let your beauty be merely external; let it come from the inside.

It's fine if you want to look attractive— until taking so much time to do that becomes a greater priority than your relationship with God. So, in other words, if your outward appearance becomes more important than your inner beauty, then YES, it's wrong. But does that make mascara evil? Or highlighted hair a sin? No. Unless you become obsessed with it. If your parents don't want you to wear makeup, it's wrong for you to do so. If fashion magazines make you discontent with the face or body that God gave you, you shouldn't be reading them. "Thou shalt not use benzoyl peroxide" is not the 11th commandment, but if you're afraid to leave the house because you've got a zit on your nose, you've gone too far.

God does care about how healthy your body is. After all, He did create it. But again, if you're obsessed with how much you weigh and you absolutely *need* to lose 10 more pounds or you'll die, that's wrong. God cares about *you.* He doesn't want you to beat yourself up or starve yourself in order to look a certain way.

Appreciate the beauty He created in you. Be thankful for both your inner and outer charm. Go back to 1 Peter 3 and see how Paul describes what beauty really is.

By the way, I have to admit, writing this devo made me curious. So I called a good friend.

"Lisa, what do you think of my nose?"

"Your nose?"

"Yeah."

"I've never really noticed your nose."

"You mean, we've met for coffee every week for two years and you've never noticed my nose?"

"Sorry. Remind me next time I see you and I'll look at it."

"So you've never been shocked by its enormity?"

"Huh?"

Maybe I didn't need that beauty article after all.

love

a special prayer   Dear Lord, thank You for the beauty that You created in me—both on the inside and on the outside. And thank You for the beauty You created around me. Forgive me for focusing too much on my outward appearance. I'm sorry for the times I've made changing my appearance more important than appreciating how You created me to be. You did a good job, God. You really did. Help me remember that. In Jesus' name, Amen.

LYIN' AT THE ZOO

The transaction was pretty easy. Too easy. And hey . . . she worked hard.

It was the scandal of the town—the city's zoo controller was caught embezzling funds. The $200,000 stolen over the previous few years allowed the woman to go on extravagant vacations and buy luxury vehicles—while other zoo employees donated their own money to feed the animals, made do with ratty uniforms, and brought tools from home because the budget was so tight.

"We feel betrayed," said one zoo worker.

What would possess someone to do that? I don't think she took the job at the zoo with the intention to steal. I believe she originally cared about the zoo and the animals. But, as the story goes, she bought a house that needed remodeling, and so as a "one-time" deal, she borrowed some funds. The transaction was pretty easy. Too easy. And hey . . . she worked hard. She didn't get paid much. She deserved it. Right?

That's the excuse she heard inside her own head. That's the lie she believed. Once she believed the lies, stealing became easier. Maybe she had a tough day and thought she could buy something online to make herself feel better. Maybe her car broke down and she justified that she needed a new SUV to get to and from work. After all, she'd earned it.

And then she admitted to the detectives that she'd become used to the nicer lifestyle. Before she was caught, she'd pretty much quadrupled her salary.

The zookeepers had sacrificed for the zoo. They'd seen animals go without their needs being met because funds weren't available to care for them properly. Yet, even in court, the zoo controller defended her position. She took the money because she deserved it. And she still believed that.

Wow.

How could she believe she deserved luxury at the expense of God's creatures going without their needs being met?

It only takes one lie.

You don't think you'd do that? Probably not. But we all listen to lies some time or another. What lies do you hear that people believe?...............

....

....

....

Here are some lies other teens have believed:

- She'll ruin you if you befriend her.

- Church kids are geeks. I'll have more of an influence on someone's life if I don't tell them I attend.

- One drink won't hurt me.

- I'm not going to go all the way with my boyfriend. I'll just let him . . .

- My parents don't understand teens today, so it's okay if I lie to them.

- I'm too tired to spend time with God. It doesn't matter if I wait until tomorrow.

- If I peek over at her paper for one answer on the test, it's not a big deal. It's just one answer.

There's a grain of truth in each of the above statements. And a lot of lie.

funds

budget

ratty

luxury

steal

funds

budget

ratty

luxury

steal

The devil knows how to use logic and strategy, moving one step at a time. He didn't tell Miss Zoo Controller to embezzle a couple hundred thousand dollars at the very start; he told her it wouldn't be a big deal to "borrow" a few hundred. He didn't tell your friend in youth group to have sex; he told her it felt good to kiss in private. He didn't tell my former high school buddy to visit prostitutes; he told him that peeking at pornography on the Internet was a good quick fix to feeling lousy.

The Bible commands us to not give a foothold to the devil. Temptations may be thrown at us left and right. Lies like the ones above and many more come at us faster than we can think sometimes. But there are ways to guard ourselves by recognizing the lies we hear.

Write down more of the lies you've heard recently that sound pretty good on the surface.

....

....

Look at what Jesus did when he heard the lies in Matthew 4:1-10. What was His strategy?

....

....

dig deeper

Look at the following verses. What are some other ways to fight the lies of the devil?

James 4:7 ....

....

Matthew 26:41 ....

....

1 Corinthians 10:13 ....

....

Ephesians 6:10-13 ....

....

love

The victory is yours. Those of us in Christ Jesus are the winners. (See Romans 16:20a, Philippians 2:10-11, 2 Thessalonians 3:3, Colossians 2:15). And throughout the Word, God coaches us in how to do battle.

Look back over the passages mentioned above. What's your strategy going to be as the lies are thrown *your* way?

....

....

....

....

....

Remember, you are not on neutral ground. You are part of a great spiritual battle. And if you are doing good work for the kingdom of God, you are a target for the devil to tempt and lead astray. That isn't something to be afraid of, but it does mean you should be prepared to fight.

What verse will you memorize to help you remember the battle and stand firm against the lies? Write it here:

....

....

....

....

a special prayer

Dear Father, thank You that I don't battle the devil alone. The victory is Yours. But it's still hard sometimes, God, to not believe the lies. It's easy to fall into temptation even when I try so hard not to. Please give me wisdom and discernment. Thank You for always giving me a way out of the temptation. Help me to take Your way and believe Your truth. Thank You for giving us Your Word to battle with. In Your name, Amen.

love

journal

SANDY

I can't be partners with Sandy. I have other problems to worry about.

She was easy to overlook. She sat behind me in English, her matted brown hair falling into her face. Her crooked teeth hid themselves behind tight lips. And she never got up during class to go to the bathroom or sharpen her pencil because it was such an ordeal for her to squeeze back into her seat. To me she was simply Sandy. To many she was "Fat Sandy."

I didn't want to be mean to her like everyone else. So I ignored her completely. I'd pass papers back to her without making any comments (although I noticed she usually received a near perfect score). I think I even smiled at her once or twice.

One day Mr. Mortensen assigned the class a Shakespeare project. We were to pair up and prepare a presentation to give in front of the class on a Shakespeare play. I looked around the room as other students grabbed partners. I heard the chair behind me creak as Sandy leaned forward in her chair. I felt a tap on my shoulder.

I wish I could say I turned around and with a big smile said, "Hey, Sandy, let's be partners." I wish I could say we worked together and had a great time and I was amazed by what a cool person she was. I wish I could say we did a great presentation together and the class loved it.

But none of the above happened.

Instead, I thought, *I can't be partners with Sandy. I have other problems to worry about.* Lisa Bernstein was throwing a party the next week and everyone who's anyone was going to be there. *If I hang out with Lisa's best friend, Callie, maybe Lisa will invite me to the party.* Ignoring Sandy, ignoring the tap, I leaned across the aisle. "Hey, Callie . . ."

Sandy ended up partnerless. Mr. Mortensen gave her the option of either joining a pair as a third, or doing a slightly shorter presentation by herself. I remember her looking around the room, and then down at her hands. "I'll do it myself."

It didn't matter, I guess. She never showed up the day of her presentation and didn't bother to make it up later. I don't know how much that hurt her grade.

I don't remember if I ended up going to Lisa Bernstein's party. But I do remember running into Sandy a few years later. Home from college for the summer, I waited on tables at a

love

local restaurant. She walked in one day pushing a baby stroller. Of course I recognized her. She'd hardly changed. Same thick torso, matted brown hair, tight lips, downcast eyes.

"Hi, Sandy," I said.

She seemed surprised that I recognized her.

I asked her a few questions about her life.

She never met my eyes. She'd gotten pregnant. Worked at a job she

fat

ignored

comments

funny

regret

fat

ignored

comments

funny

regret

hated. Never went to college even though I remember she'd had a scholarship opportunity. "I needed to stay home with my sisters. My mom doesn't take really good care of them."

I didn't ask any more. I tried to be cheery, like we'd been good chums, but we both knew the truth.

"Hey, Callie . . ."

Funny. I don't look back on my years in high school and cringe at the memory of losing my biology report. Or wonder why I chose to wear the black dress to prom instead of the red. And even though I can't imagine what I was thinking when I chose that hairstyle my junior year, it doesn't bother me. No, the thing I most regret is that day in English class when I had the opportunity to make a difference in someone's life, and I chose not to.

I'd been given the chance to be Christ to someone who desperately needed to be loved, and I had decided my reputation and a party invitation were more important. God handed me a jewel to polish and I threw it away.

Read Matthew 25:40. What does Jesus say we're doing when we love "the least of these"?..

....

We've talked a lot in this book about your value. And that's important to recognize. You're created in the image of God. You're wonderfully made. You were formed with a purpose and plan. But don't forget: so is the pimple-faced kid who sits by himself at lunch. So is the girl who wears too much makeup and is called a slut behind her back. So is Sandy.

questions:

Who are the "least of these" God has brought into your life to love? Do you recognize them, or do you choose to ignore them for the sake of your own popularity?

Ask God to show you who He wants you to love. Write their names below.

....

....

How can you love these people as God would desire you to? It doesn't mean you have to become their best friend. It may just mean showing them they are valued through your small acts of kindness.

God is love. Whoever lives in love lives in God, and God in him. In this way, love is made complete among us. (1 John 4:16-17a)

It is only God in us that gives us the capacity to love. Think about it—how would God, in you, love the people you listed above?..

....

....

....

Pray for these people in your life. And pray for wisdom and courage to love them the way you were called to love.

love

a special prayer

Lord, it is only through You that I can truly love others. Please fill me with Your love until it overflows onto everyone around me. Pour Your grace and compassion into my heart. Please help me to see people through Your eyes. Show me how precious they are to You. And help them see Your love through me. Amen.

HOW DO I HEAR GOD?

The murmurings of our busyness and disobedience hinder us from hearing God's voice.

Frank decided he was going to live a godly life, but he didn't know how. So he prayed. "God, come down here and tell me what to do." And he waited for God on his front step. Soon, his pastor came along.

"Frank," the gray-haired man called out as he approached him. "I woke up thinking about you today. I felt a burden on my heart to give you a Bible. So I went to pick one up."

"Thanks, Pastor," replied Frank.

"Do you want to sit and talk for a while?" the pastor asked.

"No. I'm kinda busy right now. I'm waiting for God to show up."

Pretty soon a little old lady walked by. He recognized her as his new next-door neighbor. The lady introduced herself.

"I'm Gwyneth," she said.

"I can't talk right now," he answered. "I'm waiting for God."

"Oh. Well, if He comes by, could you remind Him that I've been praying for someone to help me put up my shelves?"

Frank nodded.

Gwyneth walked away.

As Frank continued to sit and wait, a flyer caught in the wind landed in front of him. It announced a weekly Bible study at a local church.

"I hate litter," Frank said. He wadded up the flyer and chucked it into a garbage can.

The sun eventually set and darkness settled over his front stoop. Disappointed, Frank went inside.

"God, I waited," he said. "Why didn't You show up?"

You know the moral of the story. God did show up—just not in the way Frank expected.

God doesn't show up or love us on our terms. He comes in His own way—and that doesn't usually include writing His answer in the sky. Most often, His contact with us is through means more subtle than we'd prefer. Read 1 Kings 19:11-13. What does this tell us about the way God speaks? ....

....

....

....

To hear God, the first thing to do is clear your heart of anything that can hinder His voice— like sin or distracting thoughts. Think of it this way: When you're sitting in an auditorium trying to watch a play and there are several people around you talking, it's nearly impossible to understand what is happening on stage. The same thing happens in our hearts when there are distractions or sin in our lives. The murmurings of our busyness and disobedience hinder us from hearing God's voice. Quiet the other voices of your heart by releasing the distractions and kicking out the sin.

Okay, the other voices are gone. So now how do I listen?

Great question! There are a few ways that God tends to speak, and ways you can hear Him.

- *"You will seek me and find me when you seek me with all of your heart. I will be found by you" (Jeremiah 29:13-14a)*. Recognize God's voice by spending time with Him. Sit before Him in prayer. Be silent in His presence. Do you feel a tug at your heart? Do thoughts come to mind while you worship? Pay attention to them. They *could* be God's voice to you. Write the words down in a journal.

- *"Your word is a lamp to my feet and a light for my path" (Psalm 119:105)*. Know the Word, opening it at some point every day. It helps you fight temptation and gives you guidelines for living a godly life. More than once, I've come across a passage that gave me guidance I needed, right on the day I needed it. I don't believe that's coincidence. God uses His Word, the Bible, to speak to us. But it can't speak if you keep your Bible closed.

- *Notice what opportunities are arising or disappearing.* Have you ever heard someone say, "God closed (opened) a door"? God will speak to us in that way, too. That doesn't mean every opportunity that arises is from God, but each one is worth taking a good look at.

- *God brings people in our lives to speak His truth to us.* On numerous occasions, I've had friends offer me encouragement and wisdom that felt like a gift from God. The key is to surround yourself with godly counsel. Also remember that God's counsel will never go against His Word. If someone is truly speaking wise advice to you, it will *never* contradict the Scriptures.

Take a good look at your heart. Be honest with your worries and the decisions you're making. Write down the areas of your life in which you'd like to hear God's voice.....................

....

....

Take some time to put these before your heavenly Dad. As you pray, do you feel God speaking something to you? ....

....

....

As you read the Word, what is it showing you? ....

....

....

What are the circumstances saying? Is this even a situation you have control over? Are opportunities arising? Or does it look like doors are being shut?...

....

....

Talk to your parents, your mentor or youth pastor, and some Christian friends whom you trust. What are their thoughts?..

....

....

This isn't a formula. Sometimes God wants us to wait. By nature of who He is, we can't know everything about Him and His plans. But I hope by looking through this framework you'll see some of the ways God may be speaking to you.

Call to me and I will answer you and tell you great and unsearchable things you do not know.(Jeremiah 33:3)

It may not be in your timing or in the way you expect, but God does speak to you. Learn His voice.

a special prayer

Father, thank You for revealing Your thoughts to me. Help me to be receptive of Your words. Help me to hear what You want to say to me. God, please clear my mind of everything that is not of You. In Your name, Amen.

journal

A HUNGRY TEMPLE

It was a lie. I was hungry— very hungry.

" Is that all you're eating, Kathy?" Sherri put her dinner plate, piled high with spaghetti and meatballs, next to mine which was piled low with lettuce and cottage cheese.

"Yeah, I'm not very hungry." It was a lie. I was hungry—very hungry. Especially as I looked at that rich, meaty sauce dripping off the edge of her plate.

"But you couldn't have eaten lunch, either. You were in the library," she said.

"It's okay. I grabbed a snack this afternoon." The snack had only been a bite of an apple, but Sherri didn't need to know that.

Friends from our dorm swarmed over, filling the table, saving me from explaining my eating habits to my watchful roommate. She didn't understand my eating habits were about discipline.

Reality was that I had no idea I was traveling a very dangerous path.

I was dating a guy who only gave me half his attention. Numerous women were after his affections, and I found myself constantly competing to keep myself number one in his book. (Now I know that if a man isn't going to treat you as number one, he's not worth being *your* number one.) I thought he was worth fighting for—and that something must be wrong with me. It seemed every female on campus had perfect bodies—with mine being the only exception. Since I couldn't make myself more personable or my laugh cuter, I decided to work on the one thing I could control—my weight.

I weighed myself the next morning—115! But as I looked sideways in the mirror, I noticed I still had a pooch on my stomach, and looking down, my thighs were huge. *I bet if I were 105, I'd be perfect. Tomorrow, no apple.*

Two weeks later, Sherri followed me into the bathroom. "It just looks like you're losing a lot of weight."

"I'm fine, Sherri. Just leave me alone." I'd never snapped at her before. But I was irritated. I hadn't made my 105 mark as planned, and my boyfriend seemed to be growing increasingly distant.

I'm sure I wasn't the only one on my college campus with these thoughts and behaviors. Statistics tell us too many young women in their late high school and early college years have an eating disorder. A scary thought considering that those with severe eating disorders have a 1 in 5 chance of dying. Even though every aspect of our society exalts thinness as the benchmark for beauty, it's a lie. The truth is, starving oneself is not pretty or admirable. It's an addiction that leads to the pervasive growth of body hair, fatigue, baldness, and permanent organ damage. Doesn't that sound gorgeous?

I knew there were side effects to losing weight, but I didn't care. Being skinny had become an obsession.

One day I read a study on metabolism that lauded the benefits of making breakfast your biggest meal of the day. I thought it over. I'd hit 108 and couldn't seem to break through. If I could get my metabolism going in the morning with my lettuce meal, then I could lose more weight.

At the same time, Kim, our hall director, asked me to lead a devotional before our hall meeting. I accepted, yet her invitation posed a new dilemma. The last time I'd had my own devotions had been sometime in the previous semester. Now I had five days to become spiritual.

I decided to combine the two new goals. That week, I'd eat my lettuce breakfast and search my Bible for something poignant to share with my dorm.

And somehow in that search of Scripture, I discovered who God was again. No, I hadn't forgotten His existence, but I had forgotten what He thought of me and His desired involvement in my life. Near the end of the week, I felt overcome with God's love. And as I looked at the plate of lettuce leaves in front of me, I broke down and cried. This wasn't the life I wanted. *Please, God. Save me from myself.*

piled

dripping

bite

disorders

save me

piled

dripping

bite

disorders

save me

love

love

Look up the following verses. Read each of them over a few times. Then, in your own words, write out what God is saying to you through them.

1 Corinthians 6:19-20..
....
....

2 Corinthians 7:1..
....
....

1 Timothy 4:8..
....
....

Romans 8:38-39..
....
....

1 Samuel 16:7...
....
....

As I grew to see how God saw me, it became less and less important what my boyfriend thought, and we broke up soon after.

I spent more time with my good friends who really knew me. And for the first time, I could be honest with my struggles. They held me accountable to eating well, and constantly reminded me how much I was loved. Things didn't change overnight, but it didn't take long to realize that I was much more likeable—by others *and* myself—when I wasn't so absorbed in being stick thin. There was a whole lot more to me than my weight—a lot of great things I hadn't seen before.

I know not every girl struggles with trying to be super skinny. But chances are there is something important to you that is unimportant to God. Whatever you focus on besides how God sees you can be a trap. The best way to guard yourself against these false ideas is to learn more and more about who God made you to be—how He sees you—and surround yourselves with friends who will remind you of that.

If you are struggling with an eating disorder, or think you might be, please let someone know. A parent, teacher, counselor, or pastor can help you. And if you know someone who's struggling with anorexia or bulimia, encourage them to talk to someone as well. That's the best way you can love them—and maybe save their lives.

love

a special prayer

Lord, thank You for making my body as valuable as a temple You want to live in. I want to honor You with it. Forgive me when I don't. Sometimes it's hard not to become obsessed with the way I look. Please give me Your perspective of my body. Help me see how You see me. Show me what You think is awesome about me. And teach me how to live for more important heart things and not be consumed with outward appearances. In Jesus' name, Amen.

YOU'RE NOT ON CLEARANCE

The realtor shook her head. The house was beautiful. Twelve rooms, cathedral ceilings, huge windows overlooking the

ocean, a Jacuzzi on the rear balcony, an Olympic-sized, in-ground swimming pool. Beautiful gardens, tennis courts, a helicopter landing pad. It was easily worth the $9 million selling price. But no one was biting. Who could afford it in this economy? She looked down at the ad she'd

been working on and scratched out the nine, replacing it with an eight. Eight million. Maybe now it would sell.

Two months passed. No one even called to inquire about it. She lowered the price to seven. Then six. Then five.

It's a small town, she reasoned. *No one in the area can afford a place like this.* The price dwindled to four million. A patch of grass near the tennis courts wasn't as green as the rest. She lowered it to three. The faucet in the upstairs guest bathroom dripped a bit. Down to two. She hunted for more flaws. *Ah-hah!* The door to the theatre room squeaked— she decreased the asking price to one million dollars.

Another month passed. No bites. That morning, a newscaster had commented on the continually sinking economy. The house had been on the market for a long time. Begrudgingly, she scratched out the last zero. A nine million dollar house for $100,000.

The phone rang.

Meanwhile, on the other side of town, a man skimmed through a realty magazine. He was opening another branch of his business.

unfortunately, the first thing to drop is usually the urity factor...

Despite the slowing of the economy, his company had done remarkably well. He loved the new town he'd been living in and hoped to find something on the ocean. With nearly ten million dollars set aside to buy his dream home, he'd envisioned something with tennis courts, ocean views, and maybe even a pool. He'd hoped to find something.

Hmm. . .this place looks interesting. Sounds huge. Tennis courts. Ocean views. Yep. Maybe this is. . .what?! $100,000? That can't be much of a place after all.

He turned the page.

What if that house is you? God created you to be a young woman of immeasurable worth. Someone who is worth the "price" of being treated well. You were created to be treasured, honored, and respected by the guys you hang out with. Unfortunately, many girls only want to be "sold." They feel rejected unless someone always (and immedi-

ocean

balcony

beautiful

price

honor

ocean

balcony

beautiful

price

honor

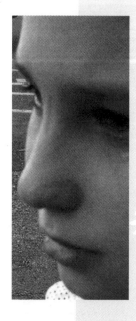

ately) likes them. So they lower their price tag. They pick out each of the tiny flaws they have and determine they're not worth the high price God intended for them. And, unfortunately, the first thing to drop is usually the purity factor. They'll start to dress less modestly and flirt profusely. You know girls like this. They probably have a lot of interested "buyers" but the buyers aren't offering much. They know from the price tag she wears they won't need to respect or treasure her. By the way she advertises her body, she makes it loud and clear she's desperate for a sale.

Unfortunately, that also means many girls miss out on guys who really *do* want to honor the woman in their lives. The men who respect a woman of purity and are willing to wait for the right one. These kind of men desire to appreciate and treasure a special girl—not just use her for their own pleasure. But when the guys see the marked-down price tag on some of these girls, they'll keep looking elsewhere for something that costs a little more. Someone that's not so easily accessible to everyone else.

questions:

What's *your* price tag? How do the way you dress, carry yourself, and interact with guys say about how much you're worth?

What's on your billboard? Are you advertising your looks or your wisdom? Your body or a kind heart? Your eye-catching fashion or your love for God?..

....

....

What do you *want* to be advertising about yourself—your value?..

....

....

How can you do that? What changes do you need to make?...

....

....

....

And what about your responsibility to help keep a guy's mind pure. *What?!* Yep, if you cause them to stumble, the Lord takes that seriously. Look up I Thessalonians 3:4-8. What are the consequences for living impurely? ....

....

Think of one outfit that you can change to be more honoring to God, to the guys in your life, and to yourself. Write it in the blank below:

God, as a way of honoring You, I commit to giving up _____.

dig deeper

Read I Corinthians 6:19–20. What does this tell us about God's expectations of our body? ....

....

....

....

love

a special prayer

Lord, You have made me incredibly beautiful and valuable. And, as my Dad, You want the best for me. You don't want me to settle for someone who only sees my outside appearance or who thinks primarily of himself. God, raise me to a higher standard. Help me be patient even when I don't have guys calling. Help me to keep my price tag high. Help me remember that I'm worth it. Thanks, God. Amen.

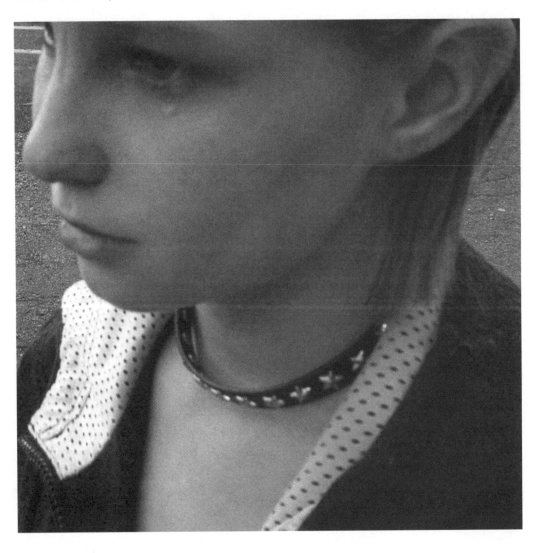

journal

SETTING THE STANDARD PART 1

"Sarah, I'm telling you. This party is going to be awesome." Greg grabbed his girlfriend's hand. "We'll have a blast."

"You know I don't like those kinds of parties." Sarah bit her lip. She and Greg had been dating for almost eight months, and everyone thought they were the perfect couple. They were both good athletes, top-notch students, and leaders in their youth group. Greg believed as long as they didn't drink, it was okay to "make an appearance" at some of the wild parties thrown by the kids at school.

Greg's voice rose an octave and he dropped Sarah's hand. "Having fun isn't a sin, y'know."

"But what about avoiding the appearance of evil?" Sarah asked.

"What about you being so uptight?" he retorted. He shook his head and stood up. "I need to get to practice. We'll talk about this later."

Sarah watched Greg's retreating back. She hated upsetting him. *Greg's a great guy. He's cute, he's fun, he treats me well. He's even a Christian. I'm lucky he chose me to be his girlfriend. Why should I be so hard on him? What more do I want?*

Derek let out a low whistle. "You look amazing," he said, awe in his voice.

Heidi smiled. She'd chosen the strappy sundress as soon as Derek suggested they picnic in the park that afternoon.

He scooted next to her on the blanket. "I can't believe I get to date the most beautiful girl at Concord High."

She sighed. "Derek . . . thanks."

"Have you thought any more about taking our love to the next level?"

"I don't know. I—"

"Heidi, you're the only girl I could ever see myself with.

...I don't want to put our relationship in neutral. I want it to keep moving forward...

We've dated for over a year. Other guys sleep with their girlfriends after two weeks."

"Just because other people—"

"That's the point, baby," Derek tucked Heidi's chin in his palm. "We're *not* like everyone else. We really love each other. I feel so close to you. And I don't want to put our relationship in neutral. I want it to keep moving forward."

"But we agreed when we signed those contracts at the youth conference that we're not going to have sex until we're married."

"Those contracts were just to make sure we don't treat having sex lightly. And we wouldn't be. Some people meet, date, and get married in a year. We'd be married by now if we weren't in high school."

"But we're not married now," Heidi fumbled over her words.

"No. But we will be someday. And I'm just as committed to you as if we were." He kissed her lightly on the cheek. "Whaddya think?"

———

"I haven't had my devotions in a week," Christi said, leaning her elbows on the lunch table.

Josh stroked her arm. "Don't worry.

hand

lip

voice

chin

lunch

hand

lip

voice

chin

lunch

God knows you're still here."

Christi smirked. "Yeah, but He probably wonders why I'm ignoring Him."

"We can pray tonight after we get back from the movie," he suggested.

"That's the problem," Christi said. "We always get back so late, and then I still have to do my homework. And then I crash. And ignore God again."

"Are you saying you want to skip out on our date tonight?"

"I'm not sure," Christi paused. She wanted to spend time with Josh. She *always* wanted to spend time with him. But she could also feel her relationship with God becoming more and more distant. And she didn't like that. "We probably shouldn't go."

"But I hardly see you. I mean between school, homework, and our jobs, I only get weekends and Tuesday nights with you. So now you want to drop Tuesdays?"

"Not necessarily all the time. But tonight I need time with God."

"You can talk with God anytime— He's omnipresent, remember? I'm not. I only have Tuesdays open. Think about how I feel."

love

Greg, Derek, and Josh aren't bad guys. For the most part, they're pretty decent.

They appreciate their girlfriends and treat them well. They're even Christians. But what's missing from the picture? Their character? Their faith? Their respect for their girlfriends?

Grab your Bible and read Ephesians 5:25-33. What does this passage say about how husbands are to love their wives? There's a lot, so read it over a few times.

....

....

....

....

....

....

The part I want to draw your attention to is how our husbands are called to love us like Christ loves the church. And how does Christ love the church? Sanctifies her, cleanses her, presents her *holy and blameless*.

Here are some tough questions for those of you who are dating someone. Does your boyfriend bring out your holiness? Does he make you feel holy and blameless? Does he draw out of you what is most godly?

....

....

....

....

....

....

But my boyfriend and I aren't married! We're just hanging out—having fun.

Saying, "I'll expect more from a guy in my life when I'm ready to get married" is like saying, "I'll get into shape once I make the Olympic team." It's the same with relationships. You have to start preparing your heart *now*. Set the standards *now*. Start expecting more *now*. If you're going to settle for less at 16, what's going to keep you from settling for less at 23? Remember, you deserve a man who is a spiritual leader and wants the best for you. Don't settle for less.

dig deeper

Look up the passages below and journal your response to God:

Matthew 22:37-38, and Ephesians 2:4-7 ....

....

....

....

....

....

Think you got a grasp on that? Imagine yourself at a slumber party with Sarah, Christi, and Heidi (from the previous stories). What would you tell each of them?

Sarah: ....

....

....

....

Christi: ....

....

....

....

Heidi: ....

....

....

....

love

a special prayer

Father, thank You for desiring the best for me. Thank You for not wanting me to settle for less when it comes to the guys in my life. Help me remember the standard You've set and hold guys to that same standard. Lord, if there is anything You want me to change in my current relationships, please show me what that is. Give me the courage to be obedient. Amen.

SETTING THE STANDARD

He wasn't someone I would marry—so why should I continue to date him?

"Hello? You've reached Men 'R' Us. How can I help you?"

"Yes, I'd like to order a man, please."

"Certainly. Have you received our latest catalog?"

"Yes. I'm most interested in Man Model #634AR."

"What size would you prefer?"

"Five foot eleven and a half. One hundred eighty pounds."

"Extroverted or introverted?"

"Extroverted."

"Religion?"

"Born-again Christian."

"Future career?"

"Missionary pilot."

"Would you like to add on any bonus features?"

"Please. I'll take the flowers once-a-week feature, and the good athlete option."

"Anything else?"

"I noticed this model comes with belching talent. Could you remove that?"

"Of course. We'll have him shipped to you in about two weeks. Will this be on Visa or MasterCard, ma'am?"

If only it were that easy.

One rainy Sunday night, a bunch of my girlfriends and I got together to write out our "guy lists." We listed the qualities of our ideal man and, when we were done, shared them with the rest of the group. A week later I broke up with my boyfriend. He was a good guy, but I discovered that night that he wasn't the right guy for me. Why? My list reminded me of the desire God had placed on my heart for certain qualities in my future husband, and this guy didn't fit my list. He wasn't someone I would marry—so why should I continue to date him? Because of who God created me to be, I need a man who loves kids, enjoys reading, and gets my weird sense of humor—and that's just the start. A guy who never wants to have kids, prefers hockey to a book, and has a different sense of humor isn't necessarily a bad guy, but he is a bad guy *for me*.

Writing detailed "guy lists" also reminded us of what we deserve: a man who treasures us, cherishes us, and desires to see us grow closer to God.

N ow it's your turn to make your own list. Remember, a "guy list" is not a shopping list. BUT . . . it is a great exercise to examine what's important to you. So try it. Here's how . . .

1. *Pray about it.* Ask God what kind of man He has in mind for you. Ask that He put the desire for that man on your heart. Ask Him to show you the qualities of that man.

2. *Think about it.* What activities are you interested in? What are the qualities in your friends that complement you and that you enjoy? What are things that annoy you about people that you'd want to avoid? What are some qualities of people that have encouraged you to grow spiritually? What is it about your dad that makes you feel safe and important? What characteristics do you think make up a godly man? Look up 2 Peter 1:5-7, Ephesians 4:17-32, Titus 2:6-8, and 1 Peter 5:5-11 for ideas.

3. *Write about it.* Have fun with this part. Don't be afraid to put down things like "plays the piano" or "really athletic" just because you don't want to make the list impossibly detailed. It doesn't mean if you meet the perfect guy and he doesn't play the piano you have to throw him back. It's a dream list. So dream, Girl! ....

....

....

....

....

....

....

....

....
....
....
....
....
....
....
....
....
....
....
....

If you need more space, just grab another sheet of paper and keep going. How big can you dream?

Now go back over the list. Put an asterisk next to the qualities that are super-important. For example, "strong Christian" should have an asterisk next to it. So should "treasures me," "respects his parents," and "sets goals for himself." (Am I giving you more ideas?) Things like "facial hair," "owns a new car," and "is a fan of the Colorado Rockies" are probably ones that aren't quite as necessary. But only you can decide that.

The asterisked qualities are your gotta-haves. These are the ones you hold deep in your heart. When a guy becomes interested in you—or you become interested in a guy—but he doesn't have all these qualities, don't waste your time. No matter how cute he is.

Offer this list to God. Remember, you're His daughter before you're anyone's wife. Put it at His feet to do with as He pleases. Maybe He'll change things on your list around a bit. Give Him that freedom. Also remember that God may call you to singleness. He may have things planned for you that you can only do while unattached. Pray about this, too—that God would help you accept being single if that's what He has chosen for you.

Okay, so I've made my list for a future guy, but what can I do now?

More than you think. Even if it's years before you meet the man you'll spend your life with, you can impact his life today—through your prayers.

This is the confidence we have in approaching God: that if we ask anything according to his will, he hears us. (1 John 5:14)

Won't it be awesome to someday tell your husband you were praying for him before you even met him? You can ask that God keep him pure, protect him, and help him grow closer to God. Write out a prayer for your future husband. ....

....

....

....

....

....

....

Check this out! Ephesians 3:20 tells us that God is "able to do immeasurably more than all we ask or imagine". Wow! Look up this verse and write the whole thing at the top of your list. Remember that God can give us more than we could ever ask or imagine. Expect that!

a special prayer

Dear God, thanks for wanting the best for me. Help me to be patient as I wait for you to bring the right guy into my life, because I don't want to settle for anything less. Today, Lord, please touch the heart of my future husband with your goodness and strength. Prepare him for me, prepare me for him, and prepare us both to serve and love You always. Amen.

love

journal

ON A ROCK AT A HARD PLACE

"You can't give up now! You're almost there!" *Easy for you to say,* I thought. *You're on the ground.*

But I was 60 feet *above* ground, clinging to the side of a rock. I had planted my palms on smooth granite, balanced my left foot on a ledge the size of a small peanut, and stuck my right foot in a crack at a weird angle. I ran my hands along the rock to search for a handhold and found . . . nothing. I loved rock climbing, but it was moments like these that I rethought that decision. My forearms had worked themselves into flimsiness, my legs were so strained they shook uncontrollably, and I couldn't feel my fingers. I wanted down.

"There's no handholds!" I called down to my belayer.

"There's a good hold about six inches above you!" my friend called.

I looked. I saw it. *Well, that's six inches too far.*

"Trust your shoes," he shouted.

Trust that my shoes could defy gravity? For the zillionth time I checked the knot that attached my harness to the rope that my friend held. I lunged off my left foot to grab the hand-hold, planting my climbing shoes vertically against the rock.

What a great move!

Well, it would have been—if I'd have made it. But my fingers missed, my shoes slipped, and there I hung. Dangling in my harness just two feet away from the rock, I swayed on the rope that kept me from falling. I took a minute to lean against the harness, catching my breath.

"Try a little to your right, Kath. Along the crack," called my heroic friend.

I saw where he was talking about, but it looked like it required more stamina than I could muster right then.

"Can I rest a minute?" I shouted.

"Take as long as you need."

Then maybe I'll get to it next week. I was tired. I'd only agreed to go climbing today because I thought it would take my mind off the decisions I had to make that week. I needed to determine my college major in five days. How was I supposed to know what I wanted to do for the rest of my

I kept going, the muscles in my legs still tight, and my fore- arms burning.

life? I wanted to do what God wanted me to do, but I didn't know what that was. And these days God stayed silent. It didn't help that I didn't feel like reading my Bible. Talking to Him felt like conversing with a brick wall. How did He expect me to make this decision without His help?

The shout came from below. "Are you ready?"

"Sure." I tucked my hand into the crack and pulled myself up. This time, I made it. I kept going, the muscles in my legs still tight, and my forearms burning. My last pull, with some unknown energy reserve, hoisted me to the top of the climb. I sat there for a moment, enjoying an amazing bird's-eye view of the mountains and rocks, a soft breeze against my sweat-drenched skin, and the excited accolades of my friends many feet below. Definitely worth it. *I can't believe I thought of quitting.*

give up

clinging

strained

sweat

climb

give up

clinging

strained

sweat

climb

In life, climbing reminds me of God. He'll let me sweat it sometimes. He'll push my limits. He'll require that I depend on Him. But if I'm harnessed to a rope He's holding, He won't let me fall.

And like the trip up that rock, if I tried some route that didn't work, He'd point out another path, guiding me to each handhold. Sometimes I'd fail. Okay, let's be honest . . . *often* I'd fail. But that didn't mean I'd ruin God's plan for me. I could take a break, dangling in the harness attached to the rope He held, rest in Him, and try again. This time maybe He'd direct me to a different path or guide me in another direction. I sometimes would get to a point where I'd say, "This is too hard. I want to give up." But He'd encourage me onward, knowing that once I got past this crisis, I'd

As I sat on that rock and waited for my friends to join me on the top, I remembered some of the big life-decisions I had to make. And, I think, somewhere in the breeze, these words met my heart: *You're not alone.*

I looked at where I was. I'd just completed an "impossible" climb. I'd never have scaled this rock without a strong rope and a trustworthy belayer. Climbing it alone would have been crazy—and most likely, fatal.

be better. I'd be stronger. And when I completed the journey, I'd be euphoric. And in heaven that exuberance would go beyond an incredible view and an accomplished goal. As we walk through those gates, we'll receive the applause of the saints and be greeted by a proud Father saying, "Well done, my good and faithful servant."

love

questions:

Do you ever want to give up? Think of a time when the Christian life felt too hard. Write it down. ....
....
....
....
....

dig deeper

God isn't just watching your life, shaking His head in disgust in the places you've gotten stuck. He is *actively involved*—even if you don't see it. Grab your Bible and find Isaiah 30:21. What is God saying to *you* in this verse? ....
....
....

God sends messengers to help us see more than we might be able to see on our own. Who are those people in your life? ....
....
....

love

a special prayer

Lord, thank You for directing my paths. It's sometimes hard to trust that You won't let me fall, but You haven't yet. You've always been there. And You always will. Lord, help me hear Your voice behind me, leading and guiding me. Give me ears to be attuned to You. Amen.

UNBURDENING

It was a perfect weekend for a three-day backpack trip. The sun was bright, the air was crisp, and the mountains were beautiful. For the first hour 11 of the 12 hikers trotted along, happily chatting.

...a lot of my worries stemmed from believing I needed to be in control...

"Is Darrell okay?" Leslie asked, looking back at our friend plodding along behind us, silent.

I shrugged. "He runs marathons. This hike shouldn't be that hard for him." But from the sweat dripping off his baseball cap, I could tell he was exhausted.

Six hours later we reached our campsite. Some of us set up tents and others of us started dinner while Darrell unloaded his backpack. Two thick hardcover books . . . a portable CD player . . . a laptop?!

Leslie's mouth dropped. "Darrell! Why did you bring all that stuff?"

He looked up unfazed. "You said we'd have time in the late afternoon to relax so I should bring a book or journal. And I thought we could watch DVDs tonight on the laptop. I brought a few options." He held up a movie selection.

When we'd planned the trip, we'd forgotten Darrell was a novice and obviously didn't know the basic backpacking rule: Pack ONLY what is necessary. As a result, Darrell's pack must have weighed far more than any of ours. No wonder he'd been exhausted.

We sat around the fire that night, eating our mac and cheese and teasing Darrell about his pack.

"My favorite show is on tonight," Leslie said. "Do you have a TV in there?"

"We're done with dinner. Why don't you get out the

dishwasher, Darrell?"

But we were also serious. "Tomorrow, when we start again, we'll split up some of your stuff. Then it won't be so heavy."

Darrell hesitantly accepted. Then he shook his head, grinning. "I'll tell you this. I've never felt lighter than I did when I took that pack off."

We said good night shortly after. I was so tired, but I lay awake. Worries bounced around the sides of my brain like a rubber ball: My aunt had found out she had cancer in the advanced stages and the outcome didn't look good. I wondered what I was going to do when I got out of college. My sister and brother had both met their spouses while in school, but I'd be graduating alone. I turned in my sleeping bag, trying to get comfortable. Leslie snored softly beside me. I wished I could get the weight of concern off me.

I remembered what Darrell said: "I've never felt lighter than I did when I took that pack off."

If only I could take all these concerns off my shoulders as easily as Darrell could take off his backpack. Hmm . . . Wasn't there a verse about that somewhere? As quietly as possible, I dug around in my

perfect

sun

crisp

anxiety

humble

perfect

sun

crisp

anxiety

humble

backpack for my mini New Testament. I found it in 1 Peter 5:7: "Cast all your anxiety upon him because he cares for you."

Sounds easy enough, God, but how do I really do that? How can I just let go of all my fears? I looked at the verse before it: "Humble yourselves, therefore under God's mighty hand, that he may lift you up in due time."

Humble myself? How do those two verses connect? As I thought about it, I realized a lot of my worries stemmed from believing I needed to be in control, thinking I knew what was best for me. If it were up to me, my aunt would have a miraculous healing and Mr. Wonderful would walk (or maybe hike since we were on the trail) into my life tomorrow. And believing I needed to be in control was a pride that had to be humbled before God. I needed to say, "God, I trust that You're in control and You know what's best for me."

I was holding on tight to my worries. Instead, I should be _casting_ them away. _Casting_ is such a great word. Peter knew about "casting" nets. He didn't drop nets off the side of the boat; he and his fisher friends threw them out as far as they could.

Okay, God. Here I am. I'm acknowledging that You can handle things better than I can. You know what's better for me than I do. And I know You care about my life even more than I do. So, here it is. I'm giving it all to You . . .

One by one, I imagined myself carrying my burdens to Him. And one by one, He took them.

Of course, the problems didn't go away that night. I took back those fears and concerns a lot. And I had to keep casting them back into God's lap. Every day. Sometimes every hour. Sometimes more often than that. Yet casting became a habit I got better at as the months passed.

dig deeper

Okay, now it's your turn. Let's take a look at Luke 12:27-32.

In verse 28, why does Jesus refer to the people as having a lack of faith?

....

....

....

What does He tell us to do instead of worrying? See verse 31.

....

....

....

What does that mean?...

....

....

....

In verse 32, what is Jesus' reason for telling us not to be afraid?

....

....

....

love

Think about it. When we release our anxieties to our Father, we have a renewed freedom—a lightness in our spirit.

What are the burdens you are carrying around right now? List them below.

....

....

....

....

....

Write out a prayer giving your burdens to Him. Come humbly before God, believing that He has "chosen gladly" to give you the kingdom, as He tells us in Luke. He desires the best for you. Your concerns matter to Him. Remember 1 Peter 5:7? Cast all your anxiety on Him. Why? Because He cares for you! ....

....

....

....

....

love

journal

BETTER THAN FLOWERS

I don't really get it. I mean, I know You're supposed to be "enough." The all-sufficient God.

August 26

Dear God,

I had an amazing summer. I had a great time at my job. I spent lots of time with friends, played lots of beach volleyball, and had lots of dates—*FOUR guys wanted to hang out with me!* My friends teased me because I'd get flowers at least twice a week.

Clint always sent red roses with a poem. Jack gave me wildflowers with an amazing card. Michael brought lavender tulips whenever he picked me up to go out on his family's boat. And Jason would often leave a random bouquet on my car. I mean, what more does a girl *want?*

I don't know. But this girl wants it. I came back to school yesterday, all pumped up after this awesome summer. Then Lisha and I sat down to catch up. She told me all about her summer in Brazil. She went as a missionary and EVERYTHING went wrong. Huge storms flooded the house they were staying in, ruining most of their materials. Their van was vandalized. And three members of her team came down with mono. And get this: *NO ONE EVEN GOT SAVED.*

I'm thinking: "Wow. That sounds horrible." But Lisha wasn't miserable at all! In fact, I've never seen her so happy. She talked about what You did in her life and the lives of her team members and others. She talked about how it was so hard at points, but she learned so much about You. Then she asked me about my summer.

Uh . . .

I mean, it was great. But it seemed so *shallow* compared to hers. And I hardly talked to You at all. I guess I knew You were there, but maybe I was afraid You would disapprove of what I was doing. I knew I shouldn't be investing so much time and emotions into guys who are fun to hang out with and give me a lot of attention—but guys I wouldn't marry. Sigh. I can't deny that I like hearing that I'm pretty and smart and fun. I like getting flowers and going on nice dates.

The funny thing is, Lisha felt like she got all kinds of affirmation this summer too. But she said it was affirmation from You.

I don't really get it. I mean, I know You're supposed to be "enough." The all-sufficient God. I've heard it a hundred times in Sunday school. And I guess part of me believes that. But You don't feel like enough. You don't hug me when I cry. You don't laugh with me until my sides hurt. I can't tell if You're listening to me when I'm trying to sort through things.

You know what I feel most of all? Guilt. Guilt about not spending enough time with You. Guilt about not evangelizing enough. Guilt about wanting to spend time with one of "my guys" instead of with You.

I know I need to get back on track. I know I need to start my day with devotions and spend more time in prayer, but it's hard. *Because I really don't want to.*

amazing

great

played

attention

shallow

amazing

great

played

attention

shallow

Do you relate to anything in this journal entry?

Underline those parts. Then write why you relate below:

....

....

....

....

....

....

September 19

Hi God,

I talked more to Lisha today. I told her I felt bad that she was being Super-Christian all summer, while I'd been Super-Heathen.

And you know what she did? *She laughed*.

She told me she wasn't a Super-Christian.

And I told her that's what every Super-Christian has to say because they're so humble.

She said that at first she resented You for taking her to Brazil because everything was so horrible. But the last month, she realized how You were pursuing her.

What does that mean?

Do You pursue me?

Lisha believes You do—she REALLY believes it. She told me to read Hosea where You tell this guy to marry a prostitute named Gomer. I guess You told him to do that so Your people would see how much You pursue them again and again.

Weird.

September 25

God,

I read Hosea and it really hit me. Every time I put something in front of You—guys, populari-ty, the way I look—it's just like the Israelites turning away from You to worship idols. You gave them so much, yet they still looked for "life" in other places. And I see that in myself. I'm looking for these "idols" to fill me up. There are many things that I've made more important than You. Yet You choose to love me even when I wander away. You love me because I'm Yours, not because I have devotions for an hour every day. Sure, You like it when I spend time with You, but not so I can check it off as being "good" for the day, but because that helps me know You.

questions:

Think about the story in the Book of Hosea. Hosea's wife, Gomer, was loved and taken care of, yet she still pursued other men. She still put other things in front of her true love. What are you putting in front of your "true love" (God)? List any-thing you make a higher priority than God: ....

....

....

....

....

dig deeper

It's pretty sad the things we put before our heavenly Father. But isn't it amazing that He continues to pursue us even when we reject Him? Look up Hosea 2:19–20. What does this tell us about God's relationship with you? ....

....

....

....

....

a special prayer

Thank You, God, for the amazing way You love me. I know I don't deserve it. I know I continually walk away from You and run after other things. But You always come after me. And You always take me back. I'm sorry, God, for being unfaithful to You. Thank You for always being faithful to me. I still wish You were in human form so we could hang out together, but I know You bring people into my life to show me Your love, too. I love You, God. I'm Your Bride. I'm beautiful and unique and priceless to You. And You know what? That's better than flowers. Amen.

DROP THE MOP

...it became too much. Face tight, she stalked into the living room...

"Shelly!" Audrey looked at her sister's muddy footprints covering the freshly washed floor. Her hands squeezed the sudsy sponge in frustration. Her sister looked back at the dirty floor. "Oops. I'm sorry, Audrey. I wasn't paying attention. Let me wipe it up for you." To Audrey's horror, the muddy footprints continued across the floor as Shelly went to retrieve paper towels.

"No, don't bother," Audrey called after her. "I'll get it." *Why do I have to do everything around here myself in order for it to be done right?*

"Are you sure? Don't you want to get ready for Dad? He should be home any minute."

"Hello! I *am* getting ready. Mr. and Mrs. Fenway are coming over tonight for dinner. I'm trying to get the house ready."

Audrey loved her sister dearly, but she could never understand how someone could be so clueless. Their father, known to most as the respected and loved Mayor Morrison, was expecting very important guests this evening to discuss the mayor's run for governor, and she wanted everything perfect.

"Dinner smells good," Shelly said.

It had better. Audrey had shut herself in the kitchen for most of the afternoon. Her back ached from cleaning the entire house that morning. *And there's still so much to do.*

She heard her dad open the front door and she scrubbed harder. This floor would shine like it never had before.

"I'm home, girls," her dad's familiar voice echoed from the entrance-way.

I hope he wiped his feet.

"Daddy!" Shelly squealed and ran to greet her father with a hug. "How was your day?"

"Great, Punkin. I can't wait to tell you about it. But first, I want to hear about your and your sister's day."

As if I have time for that now. "Cooked and cleaned," Audrey called. She should put the potatoes in the oven pretty soon. *Which tablecloth would look best in the dining room?*

Her father walked around the corner.

"Watch it. Wet floor."

"Why don't you take a break? Come sit on the couch with your sister and me."

"I really don't have time, Dad. I still need to prepare the rest of dinner and dessert."

"We could just order pizza," he suggested.

Audrey shook her head. "No, thanks." Maybe her father didn't care how important this dinner was, but she did.

Her dad watched her for a minute, then left to go talk to Shelly.

Their laughter could be heard in the living room while Audrey sautéed mushrooms. As she tossed the salad, she overheard Shelly talk about some of her school struggles and her dad offer wisdom and comfort in return. Over the sound of her peeling apples for cobbler, Audrey heard snatches of what was going on at her father's office. As the conversation continued she became more infuriated. What was Shelly thinking? *Dad's got more to worry about than one of her silly friends hurting her feelings. And plenty more to do. Why doesn't Dad go write his speech for tomorrow?* The table still needed to be set. Shelly should be doing that instead of wasting Dad's time. Her jaw clenched in frustration. Why did Shelly get away with doing so little? Why didn't Dad tell Shelly to stop yapping and come help her? It wasn't fair.

Finally, when raucous laughter started

washed

wipe

scrubbed

prepare

clenched

washed

wipe

scrubbed

prepare

clenched

again, and the kitchen clock read 6:45, it became too much. Face tight, she stalked into the living room.

Her dad noticed immediately. "Are you okay?"

"No. No, I'm not." She felt her cheeks darken as her anger escaped. "I've been working hard for hours to get ready for tonight. And all Shelly's been doing is sitting in here talking to you. She could at least help me set the table. Or toss the salad. Or something. Why is it always my responsibility to get everything done?"

"Audrey," her father began. "I appreciate what you're doing, but can you understand that it's not the most important thing right now?"

What?! Not important? What about the company coming? Or the election for governor?

Salty tears slid down Audrey's cheeks. "How can you say that?"

Her father drew her in close to himself, letting her tears stain his dress shirt. He wiped her hair back off her damp face. "You are worried about many things, but only one thing is important right now. My relationship with you. That's more significant than all the work you can do for me."

Do you recognize the story? Look up Luke 10:38–42 to read the Bible's version of it.

Is Martha more like Shelly or Audrey? What did she want to do for Jesus?

....

....

....

What about Mary? Who is she more like in the preceeding narrative? What does she want to do for Jesus?

....

....

....

Now look at yourself. Do you think you're more like Shelly or Audrey in the story? Why?

....

....

....

This might be a challenging question, so think about it a little. Why does God love you?

....

....

....

....

Did you list your skills and talents or the things you've done to serve God? Did you write, "Because I love Him"? If so, you're wrong. The only correct answer is: Because you're His daughter. That's it. He loves you because He designed you, created you, and poured Himself into you. We love Him because He *first* loved us. And there is *nothing* you can do to make Him love you any more or any less.

But there are things that you do that will please Him. Do you have any ideas what they might be? Look up some of these verses and write down your thoughts.

Proverbs 3:5-6:

....

....

....

Jeremiah 15:16:

....

....

....

Psalm 119:167-168:

....

....

....

Do you think Audrey heard what her father told her? Or was she too busy?

....

....

....

Take an honest look at your own life. Are you too busy to spend time with your heavenly Dad?

....

....

....

....

....

....

a special prayer

God, forgive me for not making time to just get to know You. I know You desire that I pray and read Your Word. But sometimes I'm more concerned about church, friends, school—all important things, but not as important as me spending time with You. Thank You for being patient with me. Draw me near to You, God. I want to hear Your voice and search Your Word. I want to know Your heart. Thank You for being the Ruler of the universe who wants to spend time with me. Amen.

love

journal

love

BEYOND CINDERELLA

...you and your family will be wiped out...

Once upon a time in a land far, far away there lived a beautiful young girl. The death of both of her parents had left her an orphan—a very poor orphan.

One day there came a decree from the King. He was searching for a bride, and there would be a contest to choose her. Lovely maidens from all over the land swarmed to the castle. But when the King set his eyes on the beautiful orphan, he knew. She would be his Queen.

It's an age-old tale that you heard before you could read it yourself. Remember watching the movie *Cinderella?* We loved seeing the poor, orphaned servant transformed into a ravishing beauty, and capturing the affections of her Prince Charming.

Here's the surprising part. Disney didn't create the story line. Neither did a fairy-tale author a hundred years ago. Guess who wrote the first "Cinderella" story?

God.

Go figure. He penned it in the Book of Esther. You've probably heard the story. Orphan Esther is selected from the most beautiful women in the land to become the bride of King Xerxes. She rose from being a poor Jew raised by her cousin to the position of "Most Admired Woman in the Land."

Read the Book of Esther when you get the chance. The whole story is only 10 chapters long. The Cinderella part is told in the first two chapters. You get eight more chapters to learn about Esther as queen. Did you ever wonder what happened to Cinderella after she married her Prince Charming? Did she grow fat in the castle eating bonbons? With Esther, there's no mystery. Her rise to queendom is only the beginning of the story.

Esther enjoyed living in the lap of luxury for a while.

Ladies in waiting catered to her, choice delicacies were brought at her command, and expensive satin sheets adorned her bed. Her husband ruled over a wealthy and powerful kingdom, and she received all the benefits of being a queen. I wonder what she thought during that time. Did she wonder why God had put her there? Was she thankful to be elevated to such a high position? Did she miss her old life under her cousin's care?

But a life of bliss could not last forever. And Esther's whimsical world came to an abrupt end when she received bad news from her cousin Mordecai. He informed her that Haman, the man second only to the king, had issued a decree that in 11 months all the Jews would be massacred. And whoever killed a Jew would be able to keep all that person's possessions. What could be worse? All of Esther's family and everyone from her old neighborhood were destined to be wiped out. But what could Esther do?

Mordecai had an idea. He sent the message to Esther: *Go before the king and plead for the lives of your people.*

Esther stared at the tiled floor, dismissing the messenger with a wave of her hand. She sunk onto the pile of velvet pil-

death

orphan

poor

bliss

situation

death

orphan

poor

bliss

situation

lows. Her cousin didn't understand. *I can't simply go to the king and ask such a huge request. Why, unless someone is summoned to the throne room, they're not allowed to enter. And if someone barges in uninvited, they could be put to death.* Unless the king raised his scepter. Would King Xerxes point his scepter at her, saving her life? Or would he punish her? The king wasn't known for letting his wives do their own thing. In fact, the queen before Esther had been banished from the kingdom for not adhering to the king's wishes. And now Mordecai expected her to go before Xerxes uninvited. She hurriedly sent a message back to her cousin explaining the situation. Certainly he'd understand. He'd want to keep her safe.

But the response in return surprised her:

Don't think that just because you live in the king's house you're the one Jew who will get out of this alive. If you persist in staying silent at a time like this, help and deliverance will arrive for the Jews from someplace else; but you and your family will be wiped out. Who knows? Maybe you were made queen for just such a time as this.

T here are two things that strike
me about Mordecai's message.

love

First, Mordecai knew the fate of the Jews was not resting on Esther's shoulders. God's will would be done, regardless of Esther's choice to participate or not. However, Mordecai believed God was giving Esther the opportunity to take part in the miracle God was going to do. God placed her in the position of queen at that appointed moment in all history to accomplish a work for His glory. Wow! And she could *choose* to be His woman or not.

What about you? Do you think it was by accident that you were born the year you were and in the family you have? Was it a random occurrence that you ended up in the school you attend with the friends you hang out with? Was it by chance you have the gifts and talents you do?

Not any more than it was a random chance that God gave Esther beauty, a godly cousin to raise her, and the position of queen.

The next question is a little harder. What are you doing in your appointed place?

....
....
....

Are you open to hear God moving in your life? Are you willing to be a part of His kingdom work?...
....
....
....
....
....
....
....

Journal for a few minutes about your life and what you believe God is calling you to do with it. Why do you think you are where you are "for such a time as this?"

....

....

....

....

....

....

If you're not sure what God is calling you to, write out a prayer asking Him to give you His

dreams for you...

....

....

....

....

God, thank You for putting me where I am for Your unique purposes. Please

a special prayer

reveal to me what You want me to do at this place, who You'd like me to impact, and what You desire to teach me. I know that it is only through You living in me that I can accomplish anything worthwhile, and I ask, God, that You would help me be willing. Thank You for loving me so much that You allow me to be a part of Your work. Amen.

love

WORK IN PROGRESS

...Forget it, I'm sick of dealing with you...

"I think God's given up on me by now."

Have you ever heard that? Or thought that yourself? I know I have. Sometimes it feels like I've messed up too many times. Or failed at one too many things. Doesn't God just ever say, "Forget it, I'm sick of dealing with you"?

Let me tell you a story.

Gwen and Todd had been saving for years to build their dream house. Finally, when they'd saved enough, they hunted for the perfect piece of land. After several weeks, they found it—several acres with a small lake and mountain views. Next, they began the process of interviewing architects to design the layout for the perfect home. As the blueprints came in, Gwen and Todd examined each carefully and suggested changes. Then they hired the best builder they could find. They visited the property every day to see how it was coming. They made certain the builders were constructing it according to the plans and using the highest-quality materials. Todd wanted a big bay window, a huge master suite, and a hot tub in back. Gwen excitedly planned out a large wraparound porch, skylights in the living room, and a regal winding staircase. They picked out the paint and went to work adding color to their home. They laid down the carpeting and tile. They purchased the furniture. They bought luxury towels for the bathrooms, selected beautiful comforters for the bedrooms, and hung expensive artwork throughout. The house was perfect—exactly as they dreamed it would be.

But as they were moving in, Todd noticed something. "Y'know, I don't really

like the kitchen sink fixtures," he said. "They are so ugly I can't stand to be in the room with them."

Gwen looked at them and wrinkled her nose in disgust. "Ewww. You're right."

They looked at each other.

"We can't live with these ugly fixtures," they said.

So they got into their car and drove away—never to return.

What?! That's crazy! No one would do that!

No? Isn't it just as crazy to believe that God performs miracle after miracle in us, making us beautiful inside, and then just gives up and decides to move on? Does God push up His sleeves and dive into your life only to decide several years later you're not worth it? That's not how God works. In the Old Testament, God forgave His people again and again, loving them completely. Sure He got frustrated and angry with their repeated sinful choices. But He never gave up.

Do you wonder if He's ever done anything in your life? If you've made a decision for Him, if you've had answers to any of your prayers (even, "no"), if you hunger for Him and hear Him speak through the Bible to your heart (even if you ignore it), then He's working in your life. Philippians 1:6 states, "He who began a good work in you will carry it on to *completion* until the day of Christ Jesus." Think about it: First of all, it says He will carry on the work to completion. That means He will keep on until the work is done. Finished. Many years ago, people wore buttons that said: PBPGIFWMY (please be patient, God isn't finished with me yet). Second, this verse doesn't say He "might" carry His work in you to completion; the Word says He *will*. Choose to believe that. Choose to follow His course for you. He hasn't given up on you. He's still at work.

At this very moment, God is in a refining process with you. He's working toward a goal in your life. He knows the woman He wants you to be, and He knows how to get you there. You may not cooperate. You may choose to do your own thing at times. But God will continually be pressing on. He's not giving up.

saving

dream

perfect

ugly

patient

saving

dream

perfect

ugly

patient

dig deeper

questions:

How have you failed God? What are some reasons you think God might give up on you?...

....

....

....

Now look up Isaiah 43:25. What does God promise you in this verse?

....

....

....

Look at your list of failures. Cross out the things that God can forgive and forget. Sometimes it's easier for God to forgive us than for us to forgive ourselves. But what does God say about that in Isaiah 43:18-19?..

....

....

Isn't that incredible?! God is doing something new in you. He's teaching you and molding you and showing you more of Himself. He's creating and preparing you for a special purpose—despite your past mistakes. And you want to know how wonderful His plans are for you? Open your Bible to Habakkuk 1:5. What else does God say to us?...

....

....

....

God's plans are still in place. He isn't happy with your mistakes, but they won't thwart His plan. He's still making plans for you and carrying them out to completion. We all have to go through making mistakes and asking forgiveness, but don't stay in a sea of discouragement. Pick yourself up and look to your heavenly Dad. He's still there. And He'll show you what to do next.

a special prayer

Thank You, God, for not giving up on me even when I fail You over and over again. Sometimes I don't like the refining process, but I do believe that You're there, and You're working on me. Don't give up on me, God. I want to grow to be like You. In Your name, Amen.

love

journal

love

STRAWBERRY SHORTCAKE AND THE TORNADO

...the preliminary winds seemed to be blowing the trees nearly sideways...

The tent camper shook like a bad carnival ride as the wind howled outside. I stared out the small mesh window, watching branches and garbage dance across our campsite. Our poor dog, George, barked vainly at the coming storm. And, crouching inside my Strawberry Shortcake sleeping bag, with eyes peering out the opening, I shook with fear.

"Kathy, we need to go," my mom called over the screaming wind.

"No!" I buried myself deeper inside my bag.

Was she crazy? Go outside? That wasn't safe. I wanted to close my eyes and wait for the storm to go away. Mom tried to reason with her fearful five-year-old, explaining that we needed to escape to a tornado shelter. With great hesitation—and a lot of tears—I eventually submitted myself to being carried to the car, where my dad and siblings waited.

The tornado hadn't hit yet, but the preliminary winds seemed to be blowing the trees nearly sideways. The campground was aptly named "Shady Lane" as the number of leaning trees proved. Before they'd been pretty; now the massive number of towering oaks terrified me. I cried during the two-minute drive to the shelter.

We survived the tornado that day, despite damage done throughout the campground. Fallen trees destroyed a number of camper trailers and tents, and injured those who'd unwittingly remained inside them. I can look back on that stormy Saturday and appreciate my parents' decision to make me leave the comforts of a cozy sleeping bag to take me to a safer place. At the time, and with the understanding of a child, I'd have rather

love

stayed hidden inside my Strawberry Shortcake sleeping bag, but in retrospect, leaving had clearly been the best thing for me.

Do you ever feel that way when God is pulling you out of your "safe place"? Many times I feel like I know what's best for me. And I'll say "No!" and crawl deeper inside my comfort zone. I don't want to go out into the storm. As God coaxes me out, I find myself thinking, "God, I thought You loved me! Why are You making me go through this?" Similar to the thoughts I had toward my mom that day. But one key factor made the difference: I trusted my mom's love for me. I didn't understand the ultimate purpose for her leading me out of my "safe place," but I knew she always wanted what was best for me.

We cannot always comprehend what God is doing or why He's doing it. Our finite minds are trying to comprehend an infinite world. But we can trust that He's a God who loves us and wants the best for us.

shook

howled

vainly

cried

cozy

shook

howled

vainly

cried

cozy

Read Psalm 23:1-4 and Isaiah 40:11. In these passages, God is described as our Shepherd. Look over these verses carefully. How does the Shepherd treat the sheep?

....

....

....

Jesus describes Himself as our Good Shepherd in John 10:11-16. How does the Shepherd in this passage love His sheep?

....

....

....

....

Read verses 14 and 16 from the above passage one more time. How do the sheep respond to the Shepherd?

....

....

....

....

Where do you need to trust God's shepherding of you today?

....

....

....

....

Even though it didn't make sense to me, I obeyed my mom's call. We need to do the same with God—even when He takes us to a place that doesn't make sense or into a situation that's frightening. He's our Shepherd. He loves us enough to give His life for us, and He knows what's best for us. We can trust Him to guide us, even if it means going into the storm. His direction will always lead us to "green pastures."

love

a special prayer

Jesus, You are my Shepherd. I know that You love me so much You gave up Your life for me. And because You love me, You lead and guide me. Lord, forgive me when I don't trust the path You put me on. Thank You that I do matter so much to You. Help me to grow in my trust and understanding of Your ways—even when they don't make sense to me. In Your name, Amen.

A CHANGE OF PLANS

Nothing that night happened how I'd planned it.

My two college roommates and I were excited to move into an apartment off-campus. And we decided a dinner party would be the perfect way to celebrate! Our guest list would include 10 close friends and—after convincing my roommates it was a great idea—a soccer player I'd been drooling over. We decided to go all out on the menu. Smoked salmon rolls as appetizers. A first course of clam chowder, followed by the mouth-watering main course of mushroom and spinach-stuffed chicken breasts, glazed asparagus, and homemade garlic biscuits. For dessert—chocolate mousse cheesecake. As I wrote out the shopping list, I could picture my crush enjoying his meal, impressed beyond words by the culinary goddess I'd prove to be. Dates were sure to follow.

The day of the party, we thought we'd begin preparing the meal early—just in case.

3:00 p.m.—Start the salmon rolls. Wait, this isn't salmon, it's imitation lobster. Do you think it will still work?

3:10—I forgot to put oregano on the list. Send Lisa to the store.

3:15—Stuff the chicken with mushroom and spinach. Um, are you supposed to thaw the frozen spinach first or not? Call Mom.

3:30—Mix the cheesecake. Wait, the mixer doesn't work. Oh, well, stick the ingredients into the blender. Doesn't work—too thick. Go next door and borrow the neighbor's mixer.

3:35—The salmon rolls don't look like the picture. And they don't taste right, either. Maybe we don't need an appetizer.

3:45—Make the soup. I can't get the evaporated milk can open. Use a stake and hammer to punch a hole.

3:50—Lisa returns from store. We don't have enough eggs. Send Lisa back to store.

4:00—Mix asparagus glaze. What does "sauté" mean?

4:15—Uh-oh. The biscuits need to bake at 450 degrees, the chicken at 400, and the cheesecake at 350. Hmmm . . . just set the oven to 400 and hope for the best. Does the cheesecake look a little lumpy?

4:30—The soup tastes like vinegar. What did we do wrong? Call Lisa on cell phone to ask her to pick up

Campbell's soup.

4:45—Cheesecake collapses. Call Lisa to pick up carton of ice cream.

5:00—Gasp! We forgot to reset the timer. Rolls are burnt to a crisp. Call Lisa to stop by the Chinese restaurant and pick up rice. Why is the chicken still raw inside?

5:15—Doorbell rings. Guests arrive. Hi! Welcome! Oh, everything's fine! Smoke? What smoke?

5:30—Lisa arrives. We motion out the window for her to bring the bags in through the back door.

5:35—Asparagus! We completely forgot to cook the asparagus. We don't have time now, everything's warm and ready to go. Microwave it. Oh, yeah. We don't own a microwave.

5:36—Brilliant idea. Iron the asparagus!

5:37—Casually stride past guests in living room with asparagus stuffed up shirt.

5:40—The chicken is still raw in the middle. We can't serve raw chicken, what if they get sick? Look! A pizza delivery guy. Follow him. Give him 10 bucks extra for giving us the pizza.

The menu that night ended up being alphabet soup, Cheese Lover's Pizza, fried rice, ironed asparagus, and ice cream. Oh,

excited

party

friends

sick

alone

excited

party

friends

sick

alone

yeah. And that guy I had a crush on didn't say much except, "Do you happen to have any antacid?" Nothing that night happened how I'd planned it.

Just when we think we've got it all figured out, nothing goes according to plan. Do you ever feel that way? At least we're not alone in that complaint. If you look through your Bible, you won't find many people whose lives went the way they expected them to, either.

If David's life had gone according to his plan, he would have remained a shepherd. Ruth would've never left Moab. Paul would've continued persecuting Christians. Each of them had plans for their lives—but they weren't God's plans. He had something bigger in mind. All of these people lived in smaller stories until God changed them to something far beyond what they could have imagined.

What if everything had gone perfectly for my dinner party? What if Mr. Soccer really had thought I was the best thing ever, and swept me off my feet? What if we ran off and got married and had soccer-playing children? That was *my* plan—but it wasn't what God had in mind.

He had something better. Besides, now that I think about it, I don't even like soccer.

I'm glad God loves us enough to know what's best for us—even if it may not be what we'd choose for ourselves. He sees your entire life—from your first breath to your last—and He knows what's best for you every minute in between. That's the love God has for you. It's not what you may expect—it's beyond it!

dig deeper

Remember the story of Lazarus? Read it again in John 11:1-46.

What was Mary's "formula" for her brother staying alive?...

....

What was Jesus' plan?..

....

What was Jesus' purpose in doing things His way? ....

....

....

Write out verse 40 below and insert your name so Jesus is speaking it to you.

....

....

....

....

Offer your dreams and plans to God. Ask Him to show you anything that you hold onto too tightly. Write them in the space below. ....

....

....

....

....

....

....

....

a special prayer

Father, forgive me for believing that I can do things better than You. That I know better than You do what my life should be. Lord, I offer to You the list on the previous page and pray that You would take the driver's seat in each of them. God, I know I'll try to take them back, but please remind me that they are Your concerns—not mine. I believe You. I trust that You love me and have a plan for my life beyond what I can imagine. Forgive me, Lord, for the times I don't believe it. Thank You, Jesus, for what You've done, what You're doing, and what You are going to do in my life. I love You.

love

journal

REMEMBER

> God, are You just sitting back in heaven using me for entertainment, letting all these things happen to me?

A little boy about five years old ran giddily through the water park, making circles around his mother and father. I'd seen him earlier that day when we'd first arrived.

"Dad, can I go on the WaterBomber?" he'd asked.

"We'll do that first thing," his dad responded, smiling.

Later he'd been behind us in line for a ride.

"Mom, can we get pizza for lunch?"

"That sounds good. We'll eat after this ride."

Now his parents had him settled onto a picnic bench, with a cheesy piece of pizza in front of him.

"Yum!" the little boy said. "Can we get ice cream for dessert?"

His dad took a bite of his own slice of pizza. "I think in a few hours that would be great."

The little boy slammed his pizza onto his plate. "But I want ice cream _now!_"

"Well, you're going to have to wait, Sweetheart," his mother said. "You can't eat too much at a time."

The little boy stuck out his lip. "You're so mean. You never let me do anything!"

———

Isn't that so much like us? God gives us blessing after blessing—sometimes answering our prayers before we even ask. Yet, when we don't get our way once, it's easy to forget all that He's given us in the past.

A few months back I made this entry in my journal:

I feel like a pawn in some cosmic game of Chutes and Ladders. God, are You just sitting back in heaven using me for entertainment, letting all these things happen to me? Or do You not even care at all? I try to do what's right, but that doesn't seem to matter to You. Why would You let me go through this time of absolute hopelessness?

Have you ever felt that way—that God doesn't care? After all, He's God. If He has the power to stop your pain, why doesn't He?

water

circles

smiling

blessing

prayers

water

circles

smiling

blessing

prayers

dig deeper

At the time I wrote the above entry, I was reading through the story of Moses and the people of Israel. Look up these passages yourself and write about what God did.

Exodus 14:21-22

....

....

....

Exodus 16:8..............................

....

....

Exodus 17:6 ....

....

....

God did some pretty amazing things, didn't He? But what was the response of the Israelites?

Exodus 16:2-3............................

....

....

Exodus 17:2-3 ....

....

....

Exodus 32:1 ....

....

....

Despite the miraculous ways God provided, the people whined, complained, and grumbled. And as chapter 32 continues you can see how they even decided to "replace" God—essentially saying He wasn't enough for them.

Then, after decades in the desert, God brings the Israelites to the Jordan River—finally on the edge of the Promised Land. Remember, this is the generation of God's people who had all been born and raised in the desert. They'd never seen a large body of water, much less taken swimming lessons! And here they were supposed to cross a very wide, rushing river. God decided to give them a taste of a miracle He'd first given their parents. As the priests carrying the ark of the covenant stepped off the shore, the waters parted. The people walked through the riverbed on dry land. But would they forget God's goodness—His miraculous power—like their parents and grandparents had?

Read the command God gives them in Joshua 4:4-7.

Why would God command them to build a memorial with stones?

....

....

....

....

....

....

questions:

Remember.

We all go through times when it feels like God has forgotten us. Like the Israelites, we forget so easily the good when life is downright bad. We forget the way God has blessed us, rescued us, and protected us. Take a minute and think about your life. Maybe you've never received manna from heaven, but God has been involved in your life. Take a minute to ask God to remind you of times that He's come through on your behalf. Think about times when He turned bad things around for good. When He helped you do something. When He protected you. When you experienced His peace. When He revealed Himself to you.

Remember His faithfulness. Remember the experiences when you've felt His presence. Remember the people that God has specifically put in your life. Remember the mistakes He's protected you from. Remember the situations He's rescued you from. Remember how much YOU MATTER to Him.

Write some of the things that have come to mind below:

....

....

....

....

....

....

....

....

Just as the Israelites built a memorial of stones, you can make your own reminder of God's faithfulness. Here are some ideas.

- Make a list of the ways you've seen God work in you and tape it to your mirror or inside your school planner.

- Think of a word that symbolizes God's presence in your life. Is it Comforter, Father, Provider, Lover? Using a permanent marker, write the word on a small stone and carry it around in your pocket.

- Tell someone. In Joshua, God commands the people to tell their children about the miracle at the Jordan. You might not have children to tell, but who else can you share God's faithfulness with? _____

What are you going to do to "remember"?

....

....

....

....

....

love

a special prayer

Lord, thank You for remembering me. Thank You for working in my life—in the past, in the present, and in the future. I want to remember You, God, and all Your works in me. Help me never to forget them. I acknowledge Your power in me. Amen.

AN ALABASTER GIFT

Her most precious possession. The value of the perfume was worth a year's wages.

What can I give Him? What gift would be worthy?

Mary tucked her long dark hair behind her ear, her eyes darting around her well-furnished home. Her family was wealthy, but nothing she owned seemed good enough to give Him. He wouldn't care about a clay pot or an ornate robe. That wasn't who He was. She slumped in the corner. *I have nothing to give Him, but He deserves so much.* He was the living God—here on earth. She felt certain of it. Others thought she was crazy, but she knew it was true. He healed. He restored. He brought life. She knew the truth of His identity every time she was around Him. His eyes knew things. His voice spoke gentleness and strength at the same time. His words released power. He'd even raised her brother Lazarus from the dead. *From the dead!* How could someone not believe? In all of the craziness of life—the disappointments, the pain, the fears—this made up for all of it. He was good. He was the only good thing she knew.

A beam of sunlight entered the crack in the doorway, illuminating the little glass bottle set carefully on the shelf above the firepit. At that instant, she knew. *Of course.*

She picked up the shiny alabaster bottle, running her fingers down the smooth surface. The bottle gleamed in the sunlight. She'd been given the precious gift by her mother, who'd been given it by her mother. Her most precious possession. The value of the perfume was worth a year's wages. It was meant to be used on a body at burial—a sign of wealth and value of the deceased. But that didn't matter now. She wanted to give Jesus something priceless, and this was the closest thing she had.

She had to do it.

He deserved it.

She placed the bottle in the pocket of her garment and raced to the house of Simon where Jesus and the disciples were eating.

love

Laughter and chatter filled the room. She knew her entrance was barely noticed. Except by Him. He looked at her. No, He looked *into* her. He always did that. She could feel His concern. Without a word, she knelt at Jesus' feet. The other men began to notice and the room fell silent. She undid His grimy sandals, removing them from dust-covered feet. She smacked the sealed bottle against the floor—breaking it to release the costly perfume. The sweet scent permeated the room. She dripped the ointment onto Jesus' feet, then rubbed it into them.

She wept with overwhelming love and gratitude, her tears mixing with the oil. He deserved so much more. But this was all she had. This gift was more than perfume. It was her heart and soul—all of her affections, all of her *self*—poured out at His feet. And then she wiped His feet clean with her long hair.

He said nothing. But murmurings from everyone else began—Judas's voice louder than the rest. "I can't believe you wasted that! Think of how much the poor could have been helped by the money we could have gotten!"

"What were you thinking, woman?"

"Obviously she wasn't. A year's wages!"

Mary refused to look up. Her eyes stayed focused on Jesus' feet. She hadn't thought of that. She'd only wanted to honor Him. Was He upset with her too? She realized how she must look—bedraggled, tear-stained, clutching a broken bottle. But she'd only wanted to love Him.

Jesus' firm hand touched her shoulder. "Leave her alone," He reprimanded them. "Why are you bothering her?" He stood and lifted Mary to her feet. He spoke, His voice filled with emotion.

"She has done a beautiful thing to Me. The poor you will always have with you, and you can help them any time you want. But you will not always have Me. She did what she could. She poured perfume on My body beforehand to prepare for My burial. I tell you the truth, wherever the gospel is preached throughout the world, what she has done will also be told, in memory of her" (see Matthew 26:10-13).

hair

eyes

gleamed

chatter

wept

hair

eyes

gleamed

chatter

wept

Mary's heart was reflected in her gift. Just as the alabaster bottle needed to be broken so the perfume could be released, Mary's heart had been broken and humbled in order for her passion and love to be released.

Are you willing to be broken before God? Are you willing to release the things that are holding you back from living a life that is completely poured out at Christ's feet?

List below the things that are holding you back from giving your all to God.

....

....

....

....

....

....

What are your fears for completely surrendering—being broken—before Him?

....

....

....

....

....

I don't think Mary thought of what she did as symbolic. I believe she responded to her heart's calling to love, adore, and sacrifice for this man she knew to be God.

What can you do to honor Jesus?

....

....

....

....

....

Judas's concern seemed good—wanting to help the poor. In that room on that day, probably many of the disciples respected Judas's argument. *What a good man, wanting to watch out for those less fortunate.* But look up John 12:4-6. What does that tell us about Judas's true motivation? ....

....

What Judas said may have made him look like he loved Jesus, but we know that Judas acted out of selfish intentions, while Mary's true motivation was her love for her Savior.

I'd like to be more like Mary than Judas, but I wonder. Am I more interested in glorifying God or receiving something for myself? Do I care more about sacrificing something for God or benefiting from Him? Is my delight in loving God or in receiving His gifts?

Take an honest look at your own life. How would you answer these questions?

....

....

....

....

....

....

....

....

a special prayer

Lord, I want to be a sweet scent to You. But I know there are things that keep me from loving You the way You deserve to be loved. It's hard to want to be broken, God, but I know I need to be. I want to love You fully and completely. Today, I give You all those things that keep me from doing that. I come before You broken, Lord, and wanting to honor You. In Jesus' name, Amen.

love

journal

SHOWING OUR LOVE

Repentance is more than confessing your sins; it's turning away from them.

Let's say your friend Patty is dating a guy named Jake. She has lunch with you one day and says, "Jake lied to me about where he was last weekend. He went out with his ex-girlfriend, but he asked for my forgiveness and said that he loves me, so I forgave him." The next day, the phone rings. "I caught Jake in another lie this morning. He told me he wasn't going to see his girlfriend anymore, but then I saw him driving her to school this morning. But he said he was sorry and that he loves me, so I forgave him." The next day the doorbell rings. Patty is in tears. "Jake lied to me. He told me he was going to take me to the game this weekend, but now he's taking his ex-girlfriend. But he said he felt really bad about it and that he loves me. So I forgave him."

What would you tell Patty?

....
....
....
....
....
....

Sometimes saying you love someone isn't enough. Your actions need to show it. God loves to hear our praises. He enjoys hearing you tell Him about your love for Him. But words only go so far. If they're not backed up by actions, they're hard to believe. God desires us to give up the sins that we keep returning to. We're in relationship with Him now, and playing around with the devil is cheating on Him.

God is a forgiving and loving God, but He is also a jealous and a just God.

Can we assume that we'll be forgiven for our sins, so we don't need to worry about correcting them? Absolutely not. God expects and desires our obedience. "If you love me, you will obey what I command," Jesus says in John 14:15.

Does this mean that every time we mess up, God decides we don't love Him? Not at all. He knows we're human and that we will fail Him—again and again. And He's far more forgiving than even Patty could be. He loves you so much. And He loves to forgive you. But the true test of our love is that we try to not sin. We try *not* to hurt Him.

Repentance is more than confessing your sins; it's turning away from them. It's choosing, as you admit your sins to God, that you don't want to do these things anymore. Not because they're not fun things to do—but because you want to love God more than your sin. As you repent, you choose God over your pride, selfishness and greed.

confession time... It's just you and your heavenly Father right now. Ask God to search your heart for any hidden sin and show you any ways that you are being disobedient to Him. Take a couple minutes to just listen. In the spaces below write down the things you need to confess. Then do it. Get down on your knees if you have to, imagining yourself before the throne of God as you pour out your heart. You're not talking to a stern, sneering judge. You are talking to your Father, who loves your heart. And He's listening.

....

....

....

....

....

....

....

....

....

....

....

....

....

According to 1 John 1:9, what does God do when we confess our sins?

....

....

What do Daniel 9:9 and Psalm 103:3 tell us about the character of God? List those attrib-
utes here. ....

....

....

....

Read Psalm 103:12 and Hebrews 8:12. What does God do with our sin?

....

....

....

Find a marker or a thick pen. Across the sins you've listed on the previous page, write in big,
bold letters: FORGIVEN AND FORGOTTEN. They are no more.

a special prayer

Dear Father, thank You for Your forgiveness. It is unbelievable how good You are to me. I want to obey You to show You how much I love You. I want to turn from these sins. I hate hurting You. Please give me the strength to overcome temptation. I know I'll fail You again, God, but I praise You for always being there and being willing to forgive me. In Your name, Amen.

ON THE POTTER'S WHEEL

She was beautiful. Annoyingly beautiful. A flawless complexion, a perfect figure, and hair right out of a Pantene commercial.

I tried to somehow melt into the folding chair I was sit-

God, why did you make me this way?

ting on. Sometimes I loved these college student functions at church, sometimes I detested them. Tonight I went with the latter. Amber (even an annoyingly beautiful name) was sur-

rounded by male admirers while I searched valiantly for some flaw in her. I'd discuss it later in the women's restroom with the other girls trying to blend in with their chairs.

"Did you see the way she flirted with Stephen?"

"You can tell she dyes her hair."

"She obviously has no brains whatsoever."

But tucked beneath the criticism would be another thought: *I'm not good enough*.

I stared in the mirror that evening zeroing in on everything wrong with me. Maybe if I just exercised more or highlighted my hair or learned to be less shy. There were things I could do. Mentally, I made the list to revamp myself.

It never worked. I never woke up transformed into a five-foot-ten-inch exotic redhead. Nope, just me. Five foot three. Dirty blonde hair. Stubby fingernails.

God, why did you make me this way?

questions: Have you ever felt that way about yourself? When?

....

....

....

Look up Isaiah 29:16. Here's the scenario: The potter is forming the pot. And the pot is saying:

....

....

Does that sound familiar?

One of my favorite places on campus is the art building. Sometimes I'll go in there just to smell. I love the mingling aromas of clay, paint, and smoky kiln embers. And I love to see what the artists are creating—bold, colorful paintings of still-life fruit dried on the easels. Countless vases and bowls of varied colors and shapes line the shelved walls.

One day I watched an art student sitting at the potter's wheel, spinning it with a foot pedal. I was mesmerized as the formless clay molded underneath his fingertips. Moving his hands up along the gray goo, the top became wider. Cupping his fingers inside, a hole formed in the middle. Indenting one finger inside left a decorative band around the rim. He stopped. The wheel spun to a halt. The vase was slightly lopsided on one side. He folded it over, put his hands in a bowl of water nearby, and started again with the same lump of clay.

Did the clay jump off the wheel and say, "Okay, I'm done now. I think I'm good enough"? Nope. The *potter* decided the pot wasn't done.

After a few more tries, my new artist friend formed a beautiful vase.

And you know what he did next? Shoved it into a hot kiln (an oven for baking pottery). Did the clay jump out of the fire screaming, "That's hot! I'm outta here!" Nope, because the *potter* decided the pot needed heat.

We are the moldable clay in God's hands. He forms us into unique works of art for unique purposes. Does it hurt sometimes? Absolutely. Does it feel like we're never getting anywhere?

Sure. Does it feel like we're sitting in a fire on occasion? Yes. But we're in good hands. And while we get our "mess" on God, He gets His fingerprints on us.

The most important thing we need to know is God doesn't make anything useless. The second most important thing to know is His forming you is a process. And not always an easy one. Being molded hurts. Being put through the fire of trials really hurts. But it's for a greater purpose. God is creating us into a finished product with a purpose we don't even know yet. Even if you're not shaped exactly how you want, remember that the Potter knows what He is doing.

God wants you to like who you are. Just as He didn't want me to be Amber. He wanted me to be me. I look at it this way: If one of my art major friends gave me a vase he had made for my birthday, and I said, "It's okay, but I was hoping for a sculpture of a pigeon," he'd be hurt. God feels the same way. He doesn't want you to look in the mirror and feel disappointment in the way He created you. He wants you to *love* how He made you. Have you heard this command?

Love your neighbor as yourself.

Jesus said it in Mark 12:31. Notice He didn't say, "Love your neighbor *more* than yourself," or "Love your neighbor *instead* of yourself." He said "*as* yourself." Which means He wants you to love *yourself,* too.

dig deeper

Do you have a favorite handmade sculpture, vase, or plate? Take a good look at it. What are the things you like about it? Write them below:

....

....

....

Are there any flaws in the artwork? Maybe a slight discoloration or a crack. But does the piece look beautiful despite the flaw? Does it still fulfill its purpose?

....

....

....

....

....

love

Despite your flaws, can you still fulfill God's purpose in you? Why or why not?

....

....

....

....

....

Read Psalm 139:14 out loud. And believe it! It's true about you!

I praise you because I am fearfully and wonderfully made; your works are wonderful, I know that full well.

a special prayer

Heavenly Father, thanks for being my Potter. You've molded and shaped me, and You continue to mold and shape me. Sometimes I don't like what You're doing. It even feels like You have to smush me back into a lump and start over. But I know it's because You're working toward a finished product that is exactly what it's supposed to be—ME! Thank You for loving me so much that You do mold me. Forgive me when I think I know what's better for me. Help me to trust what You're doing. I love You. Amen.

journal

THE BRIDE

You've never been so filled with joy as you are at this moment.

The wedding march begins, and the church is packed. You peek in from the back. It's the most incredible sight you've ever seen. Waterfalls of lilies and roses cascade everywhere, huge eight-story windowed walls boast a view of mountains out one side and an ocean coast out the other. A string quartet arranges themselves near the stage. A church has never looked so magnificent. And neither have you. The gorgeous white satin dress flows around you, a silk veil delicately frames your face. You take the arm of your father and begin your march down the aisle. In all your life you've never smelled such wonderful scents, or heard such beautiful music. You're awed by the number of people; there must be thousands—maybe millions. They're all smiling for you, some with happy tears slipping down their cheeks. You've never been so filled with joy as you are at this moment.

And then you look up front. There he is. Standing tall. Smiling broadly. Waiting with anticipation. Looking at him, every hurt and fear you ever felt is gone, never to return. A giggle escapes your grin as you realize he looks like he has to hold himself back from running to you and spinning you around. He's all you could ever imagine. His strength, his wisdom, his compassion, his heart. And, beyond what you could have ever dreamed possible, is his love for you. You've never felt so loved—you can feel its perfection permeating the immense room. Everyone can. You have no doubt he will treasure you, cherish you, and delight in you forever. The wonderful thought causes tears to spring to your own eyes. *I will be Christ's bride for all eternity.*

That's my idea of what it will be like to enter heaven.

love

Hallelujah! For our Lord God Almighty reigns. Let us rejoice and be glad and give him glory! For the wedding of the Lamb has come, and his bride has made herself ready. Fine linen, bright and clean, was given her to wear. (Revelation 19:6b-8a)

But heaven seems so far away! What do we do in the meantime—here on earth? Live like the betrothed bride of Christ—because you are. As the bride of the King of the Universe, what's expected of you? Look up the following verses, and journal your thoughts:

Colossians 3:12-14 ....

....

James 4:7-8..

....

1 Corinthians 6:19-20 ....

....

Proverbs 31:25-27 ....

....

1 Timothy 2:9-10 ....

....

Proverbs 31:20 ....

....

1 Peter 3:6..

....

love

Wow! That's a lot to live up to, and maybe you think you're not up to the challenge. A bride of Christ? Maybe you've made some mistakes in the past. Huge ones. Or maybe you feel like you'll never be "good enough" to be Christ's beloved.

But the truth is, you already are Christ's beloved. And there's nothing you can do to change that. God has already purified you. Look at that Revelation 19 verse again. "Fine linen, bright and clean, was *given* her to wear." The bride didn't have to hunt down her white garments—they were offered to her. Christ is the one who clothes you in righteousness and purity. Accept that gift! Right now pray through Psalm 51:7-10.

Father, cleanse me and I will be clean. Wash me and I will be whiter than snow. Blot out my sins as though they never existed. Thank You for cleansing me. I accept Your purifying process in my life. Create in me a clean heart, O God, and renew a steadfast spirit within me—a spirit that longs to know You better and better. Give me joy in knowing my redemption. Help me not become so "used to" it, God, that I don't appreciate it. Help me always hear You and obey.

Christ has cleansed you. You only need to live it out! Act like the bride you are. Live like you're betrothed to a King. Behave like you're living for more than the things of this world— because you are!

Write out your own prayer based on Colossians 1:10-14: ....

....

....

....

....

....

....

....

....

And as my Groom and I march out of the church to an eternity filled with all the love, joy, and wonder that heaven offers, the crowd cheers their delight. Laughter, exuberance, and celebration reign. And my Groom turns to me and says, "You are altogether beautiful, my darling. And there is no blemish in you. . . . You have made my heart beat faster . . . my bride! You have made my heart beat faster with a single glance of your eyes. . . . How beautiful is your love." (Song of Solomon 4:7, 9–10, NASB)

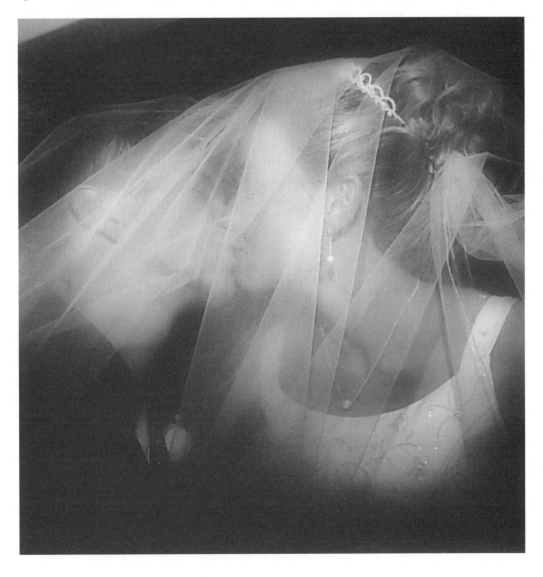

journal

journal

want more?

Want More? Life

Go from ordinary to extraordinary! *Want More?—Life* will help teen girls open the door to God's abundant life. They'll go deeper, wider and higher in their walk with God in the midst of everyday challenges like self-image, guys, godly friendships and big decisions.

Brio Girls Series

Real faith meets real life in these popular novels that give teen girls a glimpse of reality and its consequences. Girls identify with the characters as they make decisions about school and boys and learn how to manage relationships.

Bloom

Teen girls have lots of questions about life. In *Bloom: A Girl's Guide To Growing Up*, their questions are addressed and answered with the straightforward honesty teens expect and demand. From changing bodies, to dating and sex, to relationships, money and more, girls will find the answers they need.

Look for these special books in your Christian bookstore. To request a copy, call (800) 932-9123, fax (719) 548-4654, e-mail sales@family.org or write to Focus on the Family Colorado Springs, CO 80995.
Friends in Canada may write to
Focus on the Family, PO Box 9800, Stn Terminal, Vancouver, BC V6B 4G3 or call (800) 661-9800.

Visit our Web site (www.family.org) to learn more about the ministry or find out if there is a Focus on the Family office in your country.